The Kinky Murders

Jesse Stavros

Published by Trellis Publishing, 2021.

While every precaution has been taken in the preparation of this book, the publisher assumes no responsibility for errors or omissions, or for damages resulting from the use of the information contained herein.

THE KINKY MURDERS

First edition. July 4, 2021.

Copyright © 2021 Jesse Stavros.

ISBN: 979-8224821143

Written by Jesse Stavros.

THE KINKY MURDERS

JESSE STAVROS

When Sheila and Max Garvie married in 1955, they seemed like the perfect couple. She was intelligent and stunning, while he was attractive and wealthy – to everyone, they appeared to be a match made in heaven. No one was surprised when the debonair Max Garvie began courting his future bride in their small community of north-east Scotland – but no one could have anticipated the grisly end to this would-be fairy tale.

The illusion of perfection

Within the first few years of their marriage, Max and Sheila made themselves comfortable at the luxury farm handed down to them by Max's family. To fill some of the many rooms at the Fordoun, Kincardineshire, estate, the couple decided to have children – two daughters and a son before they reached the age of 30.

They had it all – a settled family life in the country with plenty of money, happy and healthy children, and a loving, committed relationship. But things started to change with the times once the 1960s hit.

There were new things to enjoy in the 60s, for those with enough wealth to afford them. Sex, drugs, and rock 'n' roll were rising in popularity faster than anyone could keep up with – except Max Garvie.

While he technically worked as a farmer on his family's property, Max had more of a managerial role – he wasn't doing much to work the fields, himself. Instead, he delegated responsibilities to his workers and simply enjoyed the profits. He was getting bored. Fast cars and a new airplane held his attention for a time, but he was restless.

Family life wasn't the perfect dream he'd thought it would be.

Max began drinking heavily. He'd also started turning to tranquilizers to try and numb his frustration – and sometimes, he'd use both at the same time. Sometimes, even, while flying his plane around in hands-free mode, performing risky moves high above the North Sea. He enjoyed the buzz that came along with the daredevil stunts, but adrenaline wasn't enough.

He needed more. He turned to sex.

No one gave it a second thought when Max ordered his staff to plant a thick triangle of trees and bushes on a section of land right next to the house. It was common for farmers to plant rows of trees in that area – the brush would offer shelter and protect the home, and the people in it, from the strong winds and weather that often blew in from the north-east.

But Max Garvie's shelter wasn't intended to protect his crops. Instead, Max had created a private area on his land where people could take off their clothes without fear of being seen – a nudist colony. He'd gotten the idea after taking Sheila and their two young daughters on a holiday in France, where they visited a nudist colony for the first time. Then, he took Sheila to a naturist retreat near Edinburgh – and when that was no longer enough, he decided to create a nudist escape of his own.

A sexual awakening

Initially, he invited only friends. It was nothing sinister, just a group of well-to-do locals enjoying a laugh together. It was the 1960s, after all, and no one was shy or self-conscious. It was a time for free love – and soon, Max started looking for exactly that.

To start, Max had orgies with small groups of close friends. Sheila wanted nothing to do with it, and refused to participate, point blank. According to Sheila, Max's sexual demands were "abnormal."

She was fine just taking care of the kids and going about their regular lives, but Max wouldn't have it. He berated her over her lack of interest in experimenting sexually, calling her things like a "fuddy-duddy," "square," or "old-fashioned." She might as well just try it, he would say. What did she have to lose? Maybe she'd even find out that she enjoyed it.

He was persistent, and eventually, Sheila gave in. And, after a few months of orgies and experimentation, she was almost as enthusiastic about her new sexual awakening as her husband was.

But despite all the precautions Max had taken to hide their private lives from the rest of the conservative community, people were beginning to notice. It's not like the couple was used to being discreet; they were flamboyant with their lifestyle – Max with his plane and expensive cars, and Sheila with her Carnaby Street fashion, tight tops and short skirts that showed off her trim, appealing figure. They weren't used to doing anything low key.

Soon, the villagers began referring to the Garvies' expansive estate as "Kinky Cottage." The community was no stranger to extreme passion, either. Just a few years earlier, a scandal had broken in Aberdeen involving a young man named Henry Burnett. He'd fallen in love with an older married woman, Margaret Guyan, who'd had an affair with Burnett but had quickly gone back to her husband, Thomas.

The jealousy drove Burnett mad, and on May 31, 1963, he broke into the couple's home and fatally shot Thomas in the face.

He grabbed Margaret and held her hostage as he drove frantically through the city. The police were right on his tail, preparing for what could have been a bloody shootout. Instead, Burnett surrendered just a half hour later.

The murder was obviously a crime of passion, but Scottish law provides no accommodation for such crimes. Burnett was hanged less than three months after shooting his lover's husband – and was the very last man ever hanged in Scotland.

Polite society in the area was shocked by the lurid details that were revealed during the course of the trial – and now, they were afraid similar things might be going down at "Kinky Cottage." They weren't wrong.

Nothing seemed to be enough for Max Garvie. Almost as soon as he broke one taboo with an orgy, he'd start looking for the next way to experiment. He was always on the lookout for something new to bring into the bedroom – or, someone.

As an officer in the SNP, Max was frequently introduced to young, handsome men. He'd had affairs with young men on his own, but when he met a 23 year old bearded mechanic named Brian Tevendale, he wasn't looking for himself. He had other plans for this attractive newcomer.

Max invited Tevendale over for tea, and for dinner, and for drinks. The young man was beginning to spend quite a bit of time visiting with the couple, but Max would often excuse himself while Tevendale was visiting. He'd leave his wife alone with this handsome young fellow for hours at a time, and after Tevendale left, he'd demand to know whether or not they'd had sex. Every time, Sheila said no, upset.

Orgies were something she and Max did together – not apart. To sleep with another man on her own, without her husband there – that would be infidelity. An affair. And Sheila wasn't the kind of woman who would cheat on her husband.

At least, she wasn't then.

Upping the stakes

Born in Stonehaven in 1945, Brian Tevendale was the last of three children born to Major Lewis Tevendale – a one-time policeman who had been presented with the DCM in recognition of his heroism during World War II. He also owned the Bush Hotel, near St. Cyrus, which was where Brian Tevendale grew up.

He first attended Montrose Academy before moving on to wireless college in Aberdeen, but dropped out after only one year, following the death of his father. Then, Tevendale made the decision to join the army.

His time there was short-lived, as well. Soon after, Tevendale was reported absent without leave, and even teamed up with a medical corps recruit to "borrow" a car.

After returning to civilian life, Tevendale managed to fly under the radar – everything was relatively unremarkable, until he and his sister met a wealthy couple named the Garvies, who owned a sprawling estate and seemed quite taken with them.

It didn't long for Sheila to discover that her husband was engaged in a sordid affair with Tevendale's sister, Trudi Birse, who was married to a policeman named Fred. According to Sheila, Max began urging her to take Tevendale as her lover, but she claimed she consistently refused.

One evening in 1967, Max Garvie finally managed to break his wife down. Tevendale was spending the night, as had become a fairly regular practice. Late into the night, his bedroom door was flung open, and – naked and shivering – Sheila was pushed firmly into the room. Max pulled the door shut and left her there.

Things between the threesome started heating up quickly, once Max had broken the ice. Often, Max and Tevendale would toss a coin to see which one of them would be sleeping with Sheila that evening – although when Max lost, he would typically insist that all three be involved, together.

Birse also began participating in four-way romps with Max, Sheila, and her own brother. Occasionally, she would even bring her husband along to join in the fun – and Max would always ensure there was another female partner for Fred to enjoy, as well.

Later, Birse bragged to friends that she and Max Garvie, known as the "flying farmer" from his days of being the most eligible bachelor in the area, had flown over the north east in his two-seater plane – while engaged in a passionate love-making session.

Things were in full swing at Kinky Cottage. But nothing was ever good enough for Max Garvie.

Easily bored, Max soon tired of his new plaything, Trudi Birse. He didn't want to sleep with her anymore, he told Sheila. So he came up with a new proposal – both he and Sheila could break things off with their other play partners and find exciting new people to bring into the bedroom. Sheila wasn't interested, and flat out refused.

It wasn't just about the sex for Sheila, Max realized. She'd fallen in love with Tevendale – and he seemed to be in love with her, too.

Max wasn't used to being disappointed. Determined to have his way, he began doing everything he could to come between his wife and the lover he'd forced her to take. At one point, Sheila attempted to run away with Tevendale, but Max tracked the couple down in Bradford and he convinced his wife to come back home. She returned to "Kinky Cottage" reluctantly – she couldn't stand being away from her children.

"May have gone abroad."

But when Sheila Garvie woke up on the morning of May 15, 1968, she found that her husband had vanished – or, at least, that's what she told the authorities. She also assured the police that nothing out of the ordinary had gone on the night before, and that she'd had no indication that he was planning to go anywhere.

Max was officially reported missing on May 19, by his sister, Hilda Kerr. She told police that the last time anyone had seen her brother was days earlier – on May 14, around 10 p.m., in Stonehaven at a meeting of the Scottish Nationalist Party. His car was found at Fordoun, parked across the runway at the flying club.

The discovery of the car led police to believe that Max hadn't fled of his own accord. Teams of investigators searched the woods in the surrounding area, and the wells were drained – but there was no sign of Max Garvie. With no leads, the police were forced to post him as a missing person, and hope that someone would provide them with the information needed to move forward with the investigation.

The details posted in the Police Gazette read: "Spends freely, is a heavy drinker and often consumes tranquilizers when drinking. Is fond of female company ... deals in pornographic material and is an active member of nudist camps ... may have gone abroad."

Just a few months later, the authorities got what they were looking for – Sheila had confessed some disturbing suspicions to her mother, Edith Watson. Whatever her motivation might have been, she told Watson that she believed that her lover, Brian Tevendale, may be the one responsible for Max's disappearance. In fact, Sheila admitted, she suspected Tevendale might have even killed her husband.

Edith Watson was a law-abiding citizen, and didn't sit on the information for long before going to the police and relaying exactly what her daughter had told her.

"My granny went to the police," recalled Sheila and Max's daughter, Wendy – now Wendy Drew. "I remember the day they spoke. I couldn't hear the words, but there was anger and my grandmother went off.

"The night before, I had been crying because I missed (Max) and, ironically, it was one of the few times I remember my mother comforting me."

By August 17, 1968, the mystery of Max's disappearance was resolved. His putrefied body, which had been bludgeoned and shot in the head, was discovered in the drains to Laurieston Castle, St. Cyrus – the hometown of Brian Tevendale.

Immediately after the body was identified, Tevendale, Sheila, and a friend of Tevendale's – a 20 year old man named Alan Peters – were arrested and charged with murder.

"My mother said, 'I won't be long, I love you!'" Wendy remembered. "It was the only time I remember her saying that. I didn't see her again until I was grown up.

"My gran and uncle Billy (Sheila's brother) came. They said, 'Your daddy's dead, he won't be coming back.' It was matter of fact, but I think they were traumatized."

What came next was a trial described by judges, lawyers, and the media as "sordid." November 19, 1968, at Aberdeen High Court, Sheila Garvie and Brian Tevendale were forced to air their dirty laundry to the world – sexual shenanigans and all. And, as the story of Max's murder began to take shape, Sheila and Tevendale began placing the blame on each other.

In Sheila's version of the events, she was woken up in the middle of the night to find her husband gone – and discovered that Tevendale had enlisted Peters' help to murder him. Tevendale, however, argued that the entire plot to kill Max was Sheila's brain child. He'd only gone along with it, he said, because he was so infatuated with her.

He even alleged that he hadn't even been involved in the actual killing – according to Tevendale's version of the story, Sheila had told him that she'd shot her husband by accident, when the gun discharged in the middle of a dispute. Then, Tevendale claimed, he'd simply helped her get rid of the body, once Max was already dead.

According to the prosecution, the murder had been planned by the couple, with Sheila persuading Tevendale to help her get rid of her husband so that they could continue their relationship without his interference. Sheila had also claimed to have suffered repeated physical abuse while married to Max Garvie, according to what she told the court.

The night of Max's disappearance, the Crown claimed, Sheila had gone to bed with her husband, as usual, after tucking in the couple's three children.

Wendy remembers going to bed early the night of May 14, 1968. Her mother was agitated, she recalled 34 years later, and had been drinking heavily.

"No matter what," she remembers her mother saying, "don't get up."

After Sheila had sex with Max and he fell asleep, she slipped – unnoticed – from under the covers and crept silently out of the room. In the early hours of the morning, she let Tevendale and Peters into the house and armed the men with a .22 rifle – her husband's gun. Then, as she watched over the scene from the safety of the bedroom doorway, her lover used the butt of the gun to smash her husband's skull before placing a pillow over his face and shooting him in the head.

With the deed done, Sheila, Tevendale, and Peters ventured back to the living room downstairs, where they shared an entire bottle of whiskey. Calmed down, they headed back up the stairs and got to work disposing of the corpse. After wrapping Max's body in a blanket, they stuffed him into the truck of Peters' car and drove together to what they hoped would be Max's final resting place – the drains of Laurieston Castle.

According to confirmation received from an insurance company, Sheila Garvie stood to inherit £55,000 on just one of Max's many policies – he had coverage on the farm, investments, and capital, as well as his life insurance.

The grisly tale was eaten up by the public, and the media was eager to share all the gory details. Church groups, in particular, used the story as a cautionary tale about how sinning always leads to pain and destruction.

"We were protected from the terrible revelations of the trial," said Wendy, who was sent with her siblings to live with their grandmother until she passed a year later, and then was fostered and lived in Lanarkshire.

"My mum's affair with Tevendale. My dad was having an affair with Trudy Birse, who was Tevendale's sister. We knew nothing about all the talk about sex and such and their lifestyle. I had known about the dugs taken by Dad – he was under pressure; he was having financial troubles."

In the weeks leading up to the murder, Wendy does remember coming across her mother and Tevendale, locked in a passionate embrace on the family's property – but when her mother begged and pleaded with her to keep it a secret, Wendy admitted she said nothing about it.

"They had to be conspiring then, to kill Dad," she said. "Over the years, I have wondered whether, if I had spoken up, I might have..."

She added that the period between her father's "disappearance" and the revelation that he'd been killed was, according to Wendy, the most defining time of her life.

"I remember sitting, crying," she said. "I remember the clothes I wore, which shoes I had on. It is crystal clear. I was so distressed. My father was painted as a manipulating monster, but as well as know, nothing is ever that black and white.

I wonder, now, just how much of it all was truth."

According to pathologist Dr. Douglas Bain, Max Garvie was killed by a gunshot wound close to his right ear, which Bain said fractured his skull. He revealed the yellowed skull to a shocked courtroom during the trial, holding it toward the jury while using his finger to show them exactly how the bullet had entered the victim's skull – and tracing the track it took to eventually reach Max Garvie's brain.

Sheila, who watched the display from her position in the dock, between two uniformed policemen, paled and turned away from the scene. Her defence lawyer, Lionel Daiches, announced that she was feeling "indisposed," and requested an adjournment. The session reconvened shortly after – the skull, and the cardboard box Bain had pulled it from, were gone.

"I was under her spell."

While the jury at the Aberdeen High Court determined there wasn't enough evidence to convict Alan Peters, the other two weren't so lucky. Tevendale was found – unanimously – guilty of committing murder, while Sheila Garvie received the same conviction via a majority verdict. In Scottish law, a majority vote is enough to move forward with sentencing.

Fortunately, for Sheila and Tevendale, capital punishment had been repealed just a few years before – otherwise, they'd likely have been hanged for committing a murder. Instead, they were each handed a sentence of life in prison.

"We knew dad was dead and mum was in prison, but we were spared all the details," Wendy said. "I remember sometimes being frightened to go to school, terrified someone would work out who I was."

During the trial, Sheila pledged her love to Brian Tevendale – even after the couple was convicted, rumours swirled that they planned to seek permission to get married while in prison. However, once the trial was over, Sheila sent a letter to Tevendale, who was serving his time in Perth Prison.

"I have decided to have nothing more to do with you, ever again," she informed him. And she meant it – the two never saw each other again. Tevendale, though, later claimed she'd only written the letter to make a point, since she'd been refused access to her three children, Wendy, Angela, and Lloyd.

"Having Max out of the way meant we could get married, and I assumed that was her motive," Tevendale admitted in his last newspaper interview, which was published in 1999. "Looking back on it now, I'm not so sure. There was a lot of money to be gained from it. And I was under her spell."

In 1978, just ten years later, both were released from prison. Once out, Tevendale got married and was the landlord of Perthshire pub for many years before deciding to emigrate to Africa. In 2003, at the age of 58, Tevendale was preparing to establish an entirely new life in Gambia – but he died in his home of a suspected heart attack before he could even leave Scotland.

"If I could go back and undo it now, I would," Tevendale said. "But when I did what I did, I was stupid and naïve, and probably thought I was in love."

Before Tevendale passed away, Wendy admitted that she'd thought about avenging her father's death – even though, before he was killed, she said Max Garvie used to tell her he was disappointed that she wasn't slimmer.

"Sometimes, when I drink whisky, I tell people I am going to kill Tevendale," she said. "It passes, but the desire is there. I still cry for my dad, and sometimes I still see him. He is happy or sad or angry, and still going on about my weight."

Sheila got married, as well – twice, in fact. She quickly divorced her second husband – a Rhodesian welder – but then married a drilling engineer named Charles Mitchell, who she lived with until he died in 1992.

"I still love her... she's mum, can't be helped," Wendy said. "But I remember, too, her coldness and that night she killed my father. Maybe, if I had spoken up..."

Wendy struggled for a long time to deal with the pain of losing her father to murder, and her mother to imprisonment. After trying things like pills, alcohol, marriage, and motherhood in an attempt to alleviate her guilt and suffering, she finally decided to write a book about her family's tortured legacy.

"I've always needed therapy," she said. "Maybe writing can be a lasting therapy to help reclaim my life. I don't really think I've had a proper life – I was married at 16, had my daughter at 18, and was separated from them more than 20 years ago. I have not seen them since. It's painful ... I have been battered by the actions of others who committed them without a thought to me."

While Wendy and the Garvies' two other children, Angela and Lloyd, inherited their parents' massive estate – worth nearly £1 million – they couldn't escape the tragic legacy that came with it. Lloyd, with a background in building, transformed the farmhouse into a modern, expansive home fit for a new family, but was unable to sell it at the low price of £749,000. Instead, in 2017, he put the property up for rent at £1,700 per month.

According to Wendy, the siblings have failed to maintain a close relationship, and even her reunion with her mother following her release from prison in 1978 was an uncomfortable event.

"She didn't want to talk about what had happened," Wendy said. "She'd rather take me to the pub."

Sheila never returned to the swinging lifestyle she'd enjoyed at Kinky Cottage – instead, she settled in to run a bed and breakfast owned by her aunt in Aberdeen (just 20 miles north of the murder scene) and continued walking her dog along the town's beach until her death in 2014. Her days of orgies and sexual experimentation – and murder – were behind her.

DEADLY BETRAYAL : THE TRUE STORY OF BELINDA VAN KREVEL

15

SARA GRIFFITH

In June 1998, the residents of Wollongong, a small town on the outskirts of Sydney, Australia, were left reeling from a brutal murder. In the coming weeks, they would discover that this senseless crime was just the beginning of a twisted saga what would leave three men dead. Australia would watch as a twisted tale of madness, violence, and revenge spewed forth from the normally sleepy town. Soon, the whole country would know the Van Krevel name.

From the outside, Jack Van Krevel was a devoted father who gave everything he had to raise his children Mark and Belinda. His wife had left them when the children were toddlers and it had been just the three of them ever since. He visibly lavished his kids with gifts and residents of Wollongong would note that the children were always wearing the latest fashion. When Mark joined a motorcycle club Jack brought him the best motorcycle he could afford and insured that all of his safety gear was top of the line. It seemed that he was doing everything he could to create a peaceful and stable world for the children that he adored. But closed doors hide many sins. And, when his children had barely become adults, the whole world would stand as witness to the results.

Belinda recounts life with her father as violent and cruel. She describes a sadist whose greatest joy came from inflicting pain and humiliation on his children. By her account, the beatings were a daily occurrence. He would savagely hit her until she could no longer stand, then proceed to kick her, only stopping when she lost control of her bowels. "He would then leave," she had remembered, "proud of what he had done." Belinda also accused him of sexually assaulting her since childhood. When Mark was on trial for multiple murder he would assert that he too had been a victim to his father's lusts.

No-one disputes the claims of abuse and Jack himself admitted to it in open court, but he denied having ever sexually assaulted his son. Questions still remain to the legitimacy of Mark's claims. The police, judge, and jury believed it to be nothing more than an attempt to garnish sympathy and hence leniency. But Belinda, despite at the time admitting that she had not ever suspected such abuse, didn't hesitate to believe her brother. For her, it was all too easy to believe.

Fear had been the one constant of her childhood. In an interview with Candice DeLong, a retired profiler for the Federal Bureau of Investigation, Belinda had said that each day held the threat that her father would kill her. DeLong had attempted to take her back, to a happy thought in her childhood or perhaps a time when she had held some love for her father. But each of her probing questions provoked only detached indifference. Even when asked what she had wanted for her future, before violence and death had been irrevocably tethered to her name, her only reply is that she had never had a chance to think about it. All her focus had been on surviving. But no matter how bad it was for her, Belinda insists that her brother had been subjected to the worst of their father's rage. It is her strongest held belief that it is this rage, and not her brother, that is responsible for the horrific crimes her brother has been convicted of.

On June 12th, 1998, the police arrived at the home of David O'Hearn. What they found was a crime scene that would undoubtedly stick with them for the rest of their lives. Mr O'Hearn was a 63-year-old shopkeeper with no previous police record. He had been struck with a wine decanter more than 40 times and died of his injuries. Instead of fleeing the crime scene his killer had remained in order to desecrate Mr O'Hearn. His hands were severed and used to paint satanic symbols on the walls and police had found Mr O'Hearn's head in the kitchen sink. Later his killer, Mark Van Krevel, would reveal the reason for the decapitation. He had intended to keep Mr O'Hearn's skull as a trophy but when it proved too difficult to clean all the blood out he had decided, in his own words, "stuff it", and left it behind. Perhaps the only mercy, if it could be called that, was that each mutilation had been carried out after O'Hearn death. While the Wollongong police had never seen such brutality it would unfortunately not be long before they saw it again.

Two weeks passed as the residents of Wollongong attempted to go about their lives, never able to shake off the shadow of fear. Then the next victim was found. Frank Arkell was a former mayor but was also known to the police in a very different capacity. He had been under investigation after being linked to cases of pedophilia and child pornography but he was murdered before he could be charged with these crimes. The scene was a gruesome echo of the brutality visited upon O'Hearn. The killer had once again used an item from the victim's home to bludgeon them to death. This time, it had been a lamp, the cord of which was found wrapped around Mr Arkell's neck. While the killer had repeated acts of mutilation none of Mr Arkell's body parts had been severed. In another departure from his first crime, Mark Van Krevel had inserted multiple needles into Arkell's eyes and cheeks.

Four Months after the nightmare had begun, police were closing in on their suspect. Before an arrest could be made, however, Mark came forward willingly. In his confessions he joyfully led police around the crime scene, explaining each action with no trace of remorse. In some of his earliest interviews, now released to the general public, he nonchalantly told police that there was no underlining motive that had led him to choose Mr O'Hearn as his first victim. The only explanation he offered in his police interviews was that he had "been angry that day" and that when he had arrived at Mr O'Hearn's door he had "just felt like killing someone". He was even more evasive when asked about his reason for Mr Arkell's murder. At one point he claimed that they had been in a relationship for over a year but never described any domestic problems. At his trial, however, he had a very different reason to present to the jury. He asserted that both gentlemen had made sexual advances towards him. This had unwittingly brought up thoughts of his father and memories of his abuse that had thrown him into a blind fury. This was all the explanation Belinda needed. While she acknowledged that her brother murdered two men in their own homes, she still sees him as the true victim. When talking to the press she would assert that what was done to Mr O'Hearn and Mr Arkell was not the fault of her tormented brother. That after years of relentless abuse he could not be held accountable for his actions and was in need of sympathy and understanding. In her eyes, the only person to blame for what Mark had become was their father Jack.

The jury was not so inclined to dismiss Mark's responsibility and sentenced him to life at Supermax, Australia's leading maximum security prison. At the age of 19, Mark became the youngest person to ever to be incarcerated at the facility. Additionally, a special notation was applied to his conviction. Mark Van Krevel, now going by Mark Valera, was sentenced to never be released.

The verdict hadn't stunned anyone but Mark's ever loyal sister. Belinda would tell that upon hearing the verdict, her first thought was of the unfairness of it all. She firmly believed, and still testifies, that she knows her brother is a good man. Some, like reporter Allison Langdon, speculate that her unceasing devotion is the only way she knows how to cope with the reality of her brother's actions. Over the course of their lives, Mark had been the only person she could trust and she is unable to reconcile her notion of him with what he has become. As Langdon put it, "I think it's easier for her to believe that (her brother is a victim) than the truth, that he is a sociopath and a serial killer."

Whatever her reasons, no amount of evidence or debate could sway Belinda from her insistence that her brother needed help, not punishment. To her, he was not the monster the courts should be seeking, but instead a helpless victim of the real monster, their father Jack. No 20-years-old, bereft and enraged at the loss of her brother, she became determined to hold her father accountable for his crimes. But it would not be the law she turned to for help.

Keith Schreiber was Mark's closest friend and was also, at the time, romantically involved with Belinda. Together, they were perhaps the only ones who would mourn the loss of Mark, the only ones who would feel the separation as anything other than a relief. Having suffered from childhood abuse himself, Mr Schreiber was also one of the few people Belinda knew that would feel the same vengeful anger towards Jack that had consumed her own life. Almost two weeks after Mark's sentencing, Belinda turned to Schreiber for help.

Belinda still claims that she never ordered nor paid Schreiber to kill her father. However, the day after she admits discussing with Schreiber her desire to see him dead, Jack was found murdered in their Albion Park home. In interviews with Ms Langdon, Belinda insists she is not responsible for Schreiber actions. He "didn't have to carry out my wishes, he chose to do that". Years later she would speculate that the murder was possibly an act of love and loyalty, not just for her and Mark, but also for her 2-year-old daughter, who for privacy reasons will not be named in this article.

On that fateful meeting, Belinda hadn't just rehashed with Schreiber the atrocities Jack had visited upon his children. She had also told him of her new suspicion that Jack had turned his predatory gaze to her daughter and may have assaulted her already. In an interview with Ms DeLong, Belinda claims that upon telling him this Schreiber had declared, unprompted by her, "That's it, he has to go," to which she had simply replied, "right". Whether it was her intention or not, the two had effectively reached their verdict. They had found Jack Van Krevel guilt and had sentenced him to death.

On the night of August 18, 2000, Schreiber slipped into the Van Krevel home through a small window in their garage. He found an ax by the adjoining door and took it with him as he crept through the halls toward Jack's room. Neither conspirator will admit to discussing it, but the method they used to carry out the murder testifies that they had presumed it would be simple and swift. The actuality proved to be far different than their expectations. Schreiber had planned to kill Jack in his sleep, perhaps thinking that the first blow would be the last. He wasn't prepared for the older man to be awake, to struggle, or to still be alive after 25 blows. Stunned and shaken, Schreiber had abandoned the ax and turned to beating Jack with a fire poker. This too proved ineffectual as the older man still fought for his life. Jack finally met his end as Schreiber repeatedly stabbed him with a knife.

In a nearby room, Belinda had cradled her daughter as she listened to the sounds of her father's brutal murder.

Throughout the whole attack, she had kept them curled up in their bed and admits that her daughter had whispered to her, "What's happening to Poppy?" Belinda's only reply had been to shush her and cover her ears. In her interview with Ms DeLong, she would confess that she had never been "so scared in her whole life" as she had been while listening to the attack. She gave two rather conflicting reasons for this. Firstly she said that she had been afraid that, should her father get the upper hand and survive the attack, he would turn his rage on her and her child next. She was certain that, if her father had lived that night, he would have killed them both. Her second reason, however, perhaps a little odd in the company of her first, was that she had no idea if it was Schreiber. Apparently, Schreiber had kept her in the dark about his intentions, to the point that she wasn't sure if it was him in her father's room or an intruder. There is no way to know what had truly been in her mind that night but her actions are undeniable. She hadn't tried to escape, to hide her child, or call for help. She simply listened until the house once again became silent.

From interview to interview she has retold the events of that night. Throughout each, it seemed that the only times an emotion would play across her face was when she spoke of what happened after her father had given his last, agonized cry. A smile, unhidden and natural, speaking of both vindictive joy and innocent relief curls her lips as she tells how the door to her room had opened. "As if someone was checking on me," she said. Checking that she was still asleep.

That she was safe. It is both sickening and heartbreaking that this is perhaps the only time she could recall someone checking on her in such a way, like a caring guardian assuring themselves that their charge is safe. To her, this is perhaps a more profound moment than any that had come before, as speaking of it still brings forth a flood of emotions. By her account, the 'unknown intruder' left without a word, and she never saw his face.

She had stayed there, with her traumatized child in her arms and her father's corpse in the next room, for 30 more minutes. After this, she had calmly left the house and driven her and her daughter to the police station to report the murder. She never checked to see if her father was still alive. When Ms DeLong asked her why she hadn't done so her only explanation was that, upon leaving her room, she had seen blood in the hallway. She "had just wanted to get out". News of the brutal slaying and the suspicious survivors spread quickly. Wollongong was again swallowed whole into a state of terror, and once more, the Van Krevel family stood at the very heart of it.

Mercifully, this time, they weren't left waiting for the culprit to be known. The day after the murder Keith Schreiber surrendered himself to the police. The reason he gave to explain the passion of his crime would be repeated, years later, as Belinda explained the complete apathy she had for hers. Jack needed to die. To revenge Mark, to save Belinda, to protect the child, Jack could not be allowed to live. Like a mantra that could keep their crime righteous instead of monstrous, the two would often repeat this. Belinda would even state that the moment she knew that she had to kill her father was when she realised he had turned his lusts onto her little girl. This is a motive that, even if true, is lost under the sheer devotion the co-conspirators show for Mark. That devotion twisted, in the eyes of officers and juries, their supposed fight for survival into something that looked very similar to cold-blooded revenge. Perhaps for them, the two things were not mutually exclusive.

When she was first questioned by police Belinda had denied any involvement in the murder of her father. In the coming days, the police found evidence that several sums of money had passed from her to Schreiber. She gave the same response to Ms DeLong as she had to police when asked why she would send the man who had killed her father money. "Why wouldn't I?" Honestly perplexed she continued to say that "It wasn't a payment. I gave it to him because I wanted to." And that, since Jack had never been a true father in any sense, there was no reason for her to care about his death or that Schreiber had killed him.

With such damning evidence against them, and their defiant belief that they had done nothing wrong, there was no way for either of them to escape a prison sentence. Keith Schreiber was given 16 years while Belinda, still insisting that she had never prompted Schreiber to kill her father, pled out to the lesser crime of orchestrating a murder and received 6 years.

Even now Belinda stands by her claim that she had no regrets over what had happened that night and any part she might have played in it, resolute that she had "without a doubt" made the right choice. She still insists on her innocence and now suggests that Schreiber took it upon himself to kill Jack because he knew that if he didn't, she would have, and he had not wanted her to lose custody of her daughter. If this is true than another tragedy can be added to those that can be traced back to the Van Krevel name. His sacrifice was for nothing. Belinda lost custody of her daughter when she was convicted and has not been permitted to see her since.

Upon her release, Belinda had been determined to salvage what remained of her life. Attempting to blend back into society she happened to meet a carpet salesman named Marshall Gould. The two hit it off and, after moving in together, Belinda gave birth to a baby boy who shall also remain nameless. The new family, ducking away from notoriety, settled into a normal life together. But the peace wasn't to last. One night in July of 2013, reportedly while watching a State of Origin football game, Belinda indulged in some alcohol while taking prescription medication. The result would be devastating. "I just remember her eyes," Mr Gould would later recall, "The color of her eyes just disappeared, just like that. It was just black."

He described how their quiet night in had been shattered as Belinda suddenly began to scream at him, threatening his life. It was such an unprompted and complete shift from her previously placid demeanor that he struggled to understand just what was happening. Stunned, he didn't attempt to stop her as Belinda left the room. He hadn't expected for her to come running back with a kitchen knife in her hand. Enraged she had attacked Mr Gould. In her drug-addled state, it is possible that she was not able to fully understand who he was. This is a notion that Gould recounted in an interview with 60 Minutes. He calmed that during her attack she called him Jack, her father's name. The assault left Gould clinging to life with six stab wounds to his arms, legs, and neck.

By some sheer twist of luck, this assault did not kill him. It had been his father, Wayne who had rushed him to a hospital in time. For months Wayne had been warning his son away from Belinda, certain that there was something very wrong with her mental health. As if to confirm his deepest fears he receives a phone call from Belinda the day after the attack. She was looking for Marshall and apparently had no memory of the night before.

At first, Marshall had done what he could to protect the mother of his child. He attempted to explain away his injuries to police by claiming that he had been mugged. It didn't take long for the story to fall apart, and while Belinda insisted that she had no memory of the event, she was nonetheless charged and convicted of assault. Throughout the ordeal Gould had stood by Belinda, staying with her even as she began her second prison sentence. Eventually, however, the strain was too much. The relationship was severed and she lost custody rights to her son.

A few weeks ago Belinda was once again released. Now with the nickname 'Belinda Van Evil' and deemed in the press to be the 'most evil woman in Australia', Belinda undeniably conjures up interest, fear, and debate. Many are divided on whether she is a victim or a predator, and that is not the only question interactions with this woman conjure up.

It had cost her freedom, the freedom of a friend, and any chance she had of a life with her daughter, but Belinda still holds no regrets over the death of her father. A smile, one that can be seen as relief or joy, pulled at her lips when she spoke of the murder on the crime show Deadly Women. That alone is off-putting but many are far more baffled with her continued faith in, and love for, her brother. Seemingly unshakable in her convictions she still insists that he is a good man. She would not even by swayed when the previously withheld details of his crimes had been reviled. After Langdon had explained each in ghastly detailed she had asked if she was afraid of him. Belinda only offered an honest look of confusion and the words, 'why would I be?'

It was this blind, or perhaps ignorant, devotion that 60 Minutes reporters wanted to test. There was one last devastating betrayal that Belinda was yet to know and it was explained to her during their interview. She was presented with a book her brother had kept as a prized possession, a well-worn encyclopedia of serial killers, one from his extensive collection on the subject. It was in this book that he scribbled some of the disturbed ramblings of his mind. The one that drew the greatest amount of attention, and had been kept from the media and courtroom, was his hit list. Arranged under the capitalized title, 'who will be my next victim', Mark had put only a few names. When Langdon had directed her to look at the second name on the list, the one under her father, there was no hiding the shock and pain she felt to realize that she had been on her brother's hit list.

But even this was not enough to sway her from her brother's side. Collecting herself quickly, but not able to keep the tears from her eyes, Belinda was swift to defend her brother. She dismissed her place on the list as him "just being angry" and repeated once more that "he's a good person". This event was scandalized in some viewer's eyes and subsequently created a flurry of activity within different comment sections over the internet. Some, while not defending her actions, were outraged that such an intimate and devastating moment was created, not in a hunt for the truth but for the entertainment of the masses. Still, others interestingly enough came to her defense as advocates for the humane treatment of the mentally ill.

Those comments opened up a world of questions into just how the public view and cope with people like the Van Krevel family. Throughout both trials, her mental health had not been drawn into question nor used as a defense. While undoubtedly her past would have left her with numerous scars that would irrevocably alter the way she views the world, there is no evidence that she had ever lost her ability to tell the difference between right and wrong, or that she didn't understand the consequences of her actions. Both of which are the cornerstones of declaring someone insane in the eyes of the law. However, when the public gather to debate the interview, it was mentioned time and again, as if mental instability could be the only explanation of her violent actions or loyalty to a confessed multiple murderer. The citizens of Australia stood divided, and probably still do, in the case of Belinda Van Krevel.

Candice DeLong, a retired profiler, and host of the show Deadly Women had a chance to interact with Belinda at length. After their time together Ms DeLong offered a new theory as to why Belinda's loyalty remains unshakable. She hypothesized that Belinda is perhaps suffering from a kind of survivor's guilt.

It is DeLong's opinion that Belinda has always been "mentally stronger than her brother". Knowing this Belinda had seen it as her duty to protect her brother and ultimately that "she should have been the one who took care of him (their father)". Lingering guilt over these supposed failures compels her to turn a blind eye to the monstrous actions of her brother. This guilt might also stay with her for another, more personal reason. That perhaps, due to her own inaction, she believes she had a hand in sending Mark upon his bloody path. During the interview, DeLong had asked Belinda what had been the first time she had realized that her brother was deeply troubled. More shaken than she had been in any other part of the interview, Belinda struggled to keep her expression placid. Her voice alone spoke of her inner turmoil. One night, when they were both very young, Mark had snuck into Belinda's room. Her voice cracked as she repeated the words he had spoken, "I think I'm possessed. I'm scared." DeLong followed up on this confession by asking where a child would learn a word like that and Belinda's automatic response was "from our father. From the things he had seen." There was no indication that Belinda had attempted to get her brother professional help after this outburst and perhaps that still haunts her to this day.

For now, Belinda is once again free within society. But there is still a lingering doubt that she is no longer a threat to those she encounters. Her assertion that if "people don't do the wrong thing, bad things don't happen to them" offers little comfort and seems to stand in contrast to the tragedies of her youth. Those that hold out hope for the little girl who survived a horrible abuse find it a positive sign that during her second incarceration, Belinda had sought out counseling services. This is not something she had done during her first stay and perhaps shows an attempt to regain control over herself and her life. While she may never again see the daughter she gave up her freedom for, she does still have a chance to reconnect with her son. It would take a lot of work to prove herself capable and safe to be around him but maybe this would be the goal she needs in order to push herself that bit further. She has proven in the past how far she was willing to go for her child and many hope that she will prove just as dogged in her pursuit to better herself for the same reason.

But there are others who believe that Belinda Van Krevel will never truly be safe to be around. Numerous people who have interviewed her, like Allison Langdon, attest to her being a charming woman who could rapidly turn into something frightening. It is possible that Belinda has already set the course of her life. One that she can never truly alter. For some like Wayne Gould, it is not a matter of if, but when Australia will once again be witness to something truly unspeakable.

CRAZY IRENE

ALLISON TARPLEY

IRENE MASLIN

Despite being a bit rough around the edges, many of the townspeople residing in the rural countryside of Mirboo North in Victoria, Australia would vouch for 28-year-old motorcycle enthusiast Paul Snabel. It was true that the young man had a penchant for reckless driving. heavy drinking, and frequent drug use; however, those that knew him best saw straight through his bad boy facade. He was often described as openly affectionate and he cared deeply for his family. People enjoyed being around Paul, despite his flaws. In fact, Paul's magnetic personality made him the sort of man with plenty of friends and very few enemies.

When Paul disappeared suddenly after attending a party at the home of Donna Randall in November 1989, his flatmate was not immediately concerned for his well being. After binging on a cocktail of drugs and alcohol, Snabel would sometimes be prone to taking off on impromptu joyrides across the open roads. Even after a week or so without any contact, loved ones did not suspect that Paul could have possibly been the victim of a violent crime. Instead, people assumed that he had finally succumbed to his vices. Suspecting that he may have careened off of a steep cliff in a drunken stupor, local authorities proceeded to conduct an extensive search along Victoria's highways.

Instead of recovering a body, police were surprised to find pieces of Snabel's most prized possession – a red and white striped Yamaha motorcycle – disassembled across several garbage dumps and dams. In the coming weeks, the abandoned pieces would prove to be the first of many clues pointing to a stunning conspiracy revolved around love lost and a callous, brutal murder, unlike anything the area had experienced before or since.

* * *

Police first began to seriously suspect foul play upon receiving a report from a farmer who had stumbled upon a lone bike engine. Though authorities were sure that the engine was in fact consistent with the model whose scattered parts were surfacing across the countryside, it became evident upon closer investigation that someone had attempted to file off the vehicle's serial number. Puzzled, investigators had little choice but to retrace Paul's steps – which quickly led them to Donna Randall and her sister, Karen.

The Randall sisters were no strangers to Snabel; in fact, it quickly became apparent that Karen and Paul had been involved in a volatile relationship for a number of years. At the time of his disappearance, the two were separated; Paul's amphetamine use was beginning to spiral out of control, and after a series of physical confrontations, she sought a clean break. However, Snabel was less than thrilled to leave behind Randall. When Karen and her young son moved to a neighboring town in an attempt to escape the toxic environment, Paul tracked down Randall's child and followed him home from school. Upon discovering Karen's new address, he left an intimidating note on the front of her door, causing her a great deal of anxiety and concern.

Nevertheless, the sisters confirmed that Paul had in fact recently attended a house party at Donna's residence despite the troubling history he shared with Karen. Afterward, he had followed the sisters back to mutual friend Rhona Heaney's home. However, the Randall sisters insisted that they had grown tired of his drunken, unruly behavior and had ordered him to leave. Though the authorities were convinced of the women's innocence in the disappearance, they decided to visit Rhona Heaney in hopes of tracking down some significant leads. Once there, Rhona corroborated the story Donna and Karen had provided; the only additional piece of information she was able to provide concerned dropping her children off at the home of Irene Maslin prior to Snabel's arrival.

Feeling that their line of questioning wasn't leading anywhere meaningful, investigators began to instead focus their attention on the recovered bike parts. By the time they had begun questioning suspects, they had recovered enough pieces to almost completely reassemble the bike to its original state. As they began to place the evidence together, they noticed a very peculiar detail; the wiring of the motorcycle had been found neatly coiled and carefully placed in individual plastic bags. As it turned out, those plastic bags were uniquely designed for the state electricity commission. Upon contacting the commission, it was revealed that the bags were not readily available to the general public. After searching through a list of employees and comparing it with the names of individuals involved in the investigation, it was discovered that Irene Maslin's husband, Jano, was an electrician with the state. Having finally found a potential suspect – however tenuous their lead may have been – the police eagerly began to investigate.

* * *

On the surface, Irene Maslin appeared to be nothing more than a typical housewife. After immigrating from Holland as a small child in 1954, she attended high school locally, worked on a farm, and eventually took on a position as a nursing aide in a nearby hospital. After giving birth to a son with a previous husband, Irene met Jano at a Rotary Club meeting and quickly fell in love. Like many of the women in her small town, she enjoyed domestic activities such as cooking and gardening. Although she did not have any children with Jano, she was a well-known maternal figure in the community and frequently served as a "carekeeper". She has a reputation for knitting jumpers and accessories for expectant mothers and newborns. Irene even held an excellent rapport with the local church. With no history of prior arrests, investigators were skeptical that a trip to the Maslin household would yield any answers to the mysterious departure of Paul Snabel.

Playing the part of an average, law-abiding couple, both Jano and Irene were initially cooperative and welcomed the inquisitive investigators to search their home as they pleased. Nothing immediately stood out as suspicious. However, when they reached the garage, they found plastic bags identical to the ones found at the dump as well as several electrical cords neatly coiled in a fashion similar to the wiring recovered from the Yamaha. Lodged in the cracks of the concrete floor, flecks of red paint consistent with that of the motorbike were discovered. Also recovered inside of the garage was a used a metal file, which was covered with remnants of the same red paint.

As evidence began leaving their home for further examination, the Maslin's attitude towards the police quickly became hostile. In contrast to their initial friendliness, Jano Maslin ultimately shooed away the authorities and, on behalf of his wife, insisted that the two had no statement to provide concerning the crime. The next time investigators returned to the Maslin residence, they discovered that the married couple had packed their belongings and left town without any indicator of when they might return. Neighbors asserted that the Maslin's had gone on a Christmas vacation, although it quickly became clear that no one had an idea of where exactly they had traveled to for the holidays.

As the search for the Maslin's began, a very different portrait of Irene was painted by neighbors and friends. The townspeople of Mirboo North, frightened of her "intimidating aura", were hesitant to cross the seemingly harmless woman. The amiable, kind-hearted persona she had presented began to disintegrate as anecdotes recounting her domineering personality and aggressive behavior began to emerge. On one occasion, it was reported that Irene had hired "big blokes" to beat a man that tried her patience. Others confessed that Maslin was a frequent drug trafficker that ran with industry "heavy hitters". According to those individuals, she openly dealt amphetamines and imported kilos of marijuana from New South Wales. Though the line between rumor and reality was hazy at best, one thing became evident; the situation that the police had stumbled into was much more dangerous than they could have initially anticipated.

* * *

Days passed without a trace of Jano or Irene Maslin. Attention shifted back to Karen Randall, who had checked herself into a local hospital because of her fragile emotional state. When questioned a second time by authorities, she broke down in tears and redacted the original statement she had provided regarding Paul's disappearance. Karen then admitted that Irene had been at Rhona's house on the day of the disappearance, directly contradicting Maslin's previous statements claiming that she had never met Snabel. Several days later, Donna Randall came forward to admit that her prior testimony had been inaccurate as well. Following the hospitalization, Irene and Rhona had begun to suspect that that Karen might be talking to authorities. In an attempt to intimidate the Randall sisters, Heaney and Maslin had fetched Donna in the dead of night and ordered her to keep her sister quiet. Insinuating that their lives may be in danger if they failed to oblige, Donna made the decision to cooperate with police in exchange for safety from her friends turned tormentors.

Just a few days before Paul's disappearance, the Randall sisters had shared afternoon tea with Rhona and Irene. At that time, Karen confided in her friends her concerns regarding the increasingly unstable affair she shared with Snabel. Disgusted by Snabel's behavior, the women began discussing possible solutions to Karen's recurring relationship issues. When someone suggested in jest that they simply kill the man, Irene Maslin in particular latched onto the idea and refused to let go. The master manipulator then goaded the three women into a sinister murder plot.

Following Donna's party, Karen baited the inebriated Snabel into visiting Rhona Heaney's secluded countryside home with promises of rekindling the bond they once shared. Upon his arrival, he was instead greeted by Irene and Rhona, who coerced him into taking some drugs. The women had assured him that the syringes they offered were filled with speed; however, they failed to mention that the amphetamines were laced with corrosive battery acid. Being fully aware that the concentrated sulfuric acid would quickly wreak havoc on Paul's body and result in a gruesome death, Karen and Donna opted to leave Rhona's home once the substance began flowing through his veins. Though neither sister had witnessed the death or viewed the corpse, they hadn't heard from him following the events at the Heaney household. Several days later, Rhona and Irene mentioned having sold the couch Paul sat on because they were unable to remove the stains he left behind. In addition, Irene had organized and constructed the stories each woman provided to officers upon investigation.

Using the information Donna provided, police continued to pursue the Maslin's with new fervor. With a new lead on the location of their vacation getaway, they anxiously arrived at an address in the sparsely populated countryside. Instead of finding their suspects, authorities were greeted by Ian GIllin, an ex-footballer who happened to be friends with the women in question. When asked about his whereabouts during the time of the disappearance, he immediately admitted that he had been with the Maslin's on the day of the crime. He claimed to have spent the day digging the foundation for a new swimming pool in the backyard, and had only briefly met Paul. That evening, Jano Maslin left the property for several hours, then returned with the red and white Yamaha motorcycle. Ian was then ordered to disassemble the bike, and being a simple man, he helped without much question. Jano and Ian then proceeded to scatter the parts of the motorcycle across several dumps, dams, and bushes nearby. Matching the locations of the recovered Yamaha with the locations Ian Gillin referenced in his testimony, it became clear that he was, in fact, the person behind the destruction of Paul Snabel's bike.

With enough damning evidence in their hands to be sure of the women's involvement in Snabel's disappearance, warrants for the arrests of Irene Maslin and Rhona Heaney were filed. When they eventually returned home after their holiday vacation, they were promptly taken into custody.

The two women were reacting to the circumstances in drastically different ways. On one hand, Irene's attitude upon being taken into the station could best be described as contemptuous. As investigators began asking questions concerning the crime, she remained silent and steady. Her stony face showed no signs of guilt or remorse, though it was clear that she had something to hide. Rhona, on the other hand, was anxious and initially hesitant to confirm or deny the truthfulness of her original statements to police. Without letting much time pass, she came to the conclusion that she could not escape punishment. Unwilling to take all of the blame for the heinous crime, she agreed to provide further details regarding the last moments of Paul Snabel's short life.

* * *

Hours after the initial injection of battery acid, it appeared that the poison was not especially effective; rather than collapsing or writhing in pain, Paul continued about his business and even began riding his motorcycle around Heaney's backyard. Frustrated by their failure, the women were forced plan a different course of action. As Snabel remained completely oblivious to the women's evil intentions, Irene made arrangements for Ian Gillin to be dropped off at Rhona's home. There, the two men met for the first time and shared a drink or two. About a half hour into Ian's visit, Maslin pulled the young man aside and informed him that Paul "had to go". She then handed Gillin a child's metal baseball bat and badgered him into hitting Snabel across the head with it. Although the two barely knew each other, Gillin agreed to it out of fear. Immediately, the blow knocked Paul unconscious; during that time, the women forced another dose of battery acid into his body.

Evidently, that wasn't enough to kill him. As Paul began to moan and groan in pain, Irene began to scream at Ian to continue hitting the severely injured man. Startled, Ian Gillin swung the bat several times, fracturing Snabel's skull and splattering blood across the room. Horrified by his own actions, he became sick and stepped away from the battered, dying man. Rhona, equally horrified by the gruesome turn of events, witnessed Irene finish Paul off once and for all. Incredibly, after sustaining a number of hits to the head, he continued to cling to life and gasp for breath. Irene proceeded to grab a plastic bag, place it over the man's bloodied head, and secure it into place with a rubber band. Together, Rhona and Irene watched as their defenseless victim slowly suffocated.

Once the deed was done, Irene's husband and Ian set to work on disposing of the bike. Meanwhile, Irene and Rhona wrapped the body in a plastic tarp and unceremoniously shoved it into the back seat of their Subaru. The two women then drove deep into the isolated bushlands and dumped the corpse far from the nearest town. They also carefully disposed of all of the incriminating evidence involved in the murder.

As the police followed up on Rhona's account, the mystery finally began to gain some clarity. After tracking down Ian GIllin, he confirmed Heaney's version of events. He added crucial details regarding the intimidation tactics Irene employed; when he initially pulled away from the metal baseball bat, Maslin assured him that Paul would kill Karen unless Ian took initiative and killed him first. When Gillin continued to show reservations about murdering Snabel, Maslin began to imply that Ian might find himself in trouble if he did not do as Irene commanded. Asserting that his actions were a measure of self-defense against Irene's wrath, he had no issues taking responsibility for the crime he had committed.

Forensic teams later lifted the lining of Rhona Heaney's living room carpet and found blood stains soaked deep into the base of the floor. Unfortunately, at the time DNA testing was not readily available, making it impossible to know for sure whether or not the blood found beneath the carpet belonged to Paul. Luckily, DNA proof was not necessary for charging the criminals or discovering the fate of Paul Snabel. Using Rhona's account of where the body was dumped, police uncovered scraps of torn clothing and fragments of a human skeleton in the bush. There, they were lucky enough to recover an intact skull and jawbone; Snabel's dental records matched that of the skeleton, finally providing conclusive evidence for family and friends as to where Paul had disappeared to for so many months

* * *

After a bizarre and tumultuous investigation, prosecutors were finally able to take the case to trial and present their evidence to a stunned jury. Although Karen Randall was the impetus behind the murder, she ultimately only received two years in prison for her involvement in the plot to kill her former lover. Her sister, Donna, was awarded an identical sentence. Ian Gillin was charged and found guilty of manslaughter. He served three years behind bars before earning his freedom. The court was much less lenient when it came to jailing Rhona Heaney; she was sentenced to 10 years in prison for the conspiracy. Although her husband Jano was acquitted of any involvement in the crime, Irene eventually confessed to being guilty of murder after spending months in denial. In accordance with Australian law at the time, she received the maximum jail sentence of 15 years.

Irene Maslin has since served her time and has been released from prison. Despite her distinct lack of remorse, nothing could prevent her from being allowed back into the general public. Although her current whereabouts are unknown, her reputation has lived on. The barbarism of her action attracted plenty of media attention, and she has been featured on a number of true crime television shows throughout the years. But perhaps the biggest impact she has made lies deep in the hearts of those that were once close to her. Years after the crime, locals still recall the chills she sent shivering down the spines of her neighbors. Some authorities even likened the magnitude of her evil to infamous serial killer Charles Manson.

With Maslin having assumed a new identity, it's almost impossible to know for certain what drove her lust for blood. Perhaps she was genuinely concerned for the safety of Karen Randall; others hypothesize that Paul Snabel's drug habit may have landed him in debt. Irene may have just been seeking the adrenaline high that comes with taking a life. While her motives cannot be conclusively determined, there is an age old lesson to be learned from the tragedy that unfolded in Mirboo North. Though Irene Maslin appeared to be nothing more than an innocent housewife to some, in reality, she was capable committing savage acts – proving that sometimes, the people we hold in the highest regard turn out to be the people we know the least.

AILEEN WUORNOS

Aileen Wuornos, touted as "America's first female serial killer", shot at least seven middle-aged men to death in Florida between December 1989 and September 1990. Their bodies were discovered along Florida's northern and central highways. A self-professed hater of humans, her troubled upbringing and difficult lifestyle contributed to her demise. She confessed to six murders, claiming that she killed her victims in self-defense after they attempted to sexually assault her while she worked as a highway prostitute; however, she later recanted five of her self-defense claims, instead pleading guilty to first-degree murder in order to "get right with God." Wuornos subsequently petitioned the Florida Supreme Court to stop all of her appeals so she could die. She asserted that she would definitely kill again and felt it better that her life was ended.

Within two weeks of her arrest, Wuornos, her attorney, and the investigators in the case had already sold movie rights to her story. As such, her case resulted in several movies, books, songs, television portrayals, and even an opera on her life.

She was executed by lethal injection on 9 October 2002.

Due to the considerable media attention about her case, many published accounts actually contain considerable myth and hyperbole. Nevertheless, she remains intriguing, repellant, and "strangely pathetic".

Early Life

Aileen Wuornos was born Aileen Carol Pittman on 29 February 1956, in Rochester, Michigan. Her mother, Diane, was 15 years old when she married Wuornos' father, Leo Dale Pittman, on 3 June 1954. Two months before Wuornos was born—and less than two years after they married—her mother filed for divorce. Wuornos' older brother Keith was born in February 1955. Throughout her adult life, Wuornos went by "Lee".

Wuornos' father was incarcerated for rape and attempted murder of a seven-year-old girl. Thus, Wuornos had never met him. Leo was considered to be schizophrenic and a sociopath, and was oft-convicted of sex crimes against children thus leading to repeated incarcerations in prison. He ultimately hanged himself in Kansas' Fort Leavenworth Prison in 1969.

Diane found single motherhood unbearable and in 1960, when Wuornos was almost four years old, she mother abandoned both of her children, leaving them with their maternal grandparents, Lauri and Britta Wuornos, who legally adopted the siblings on 18 March 1960. In fact, both children believed that their grandparents were actually their parents. Wuornos would discover the truth at the age of 12 and the revelation did not help an already difficult and troubled situation.

While in school at age 11, Wuornos would trade sexual favors in exchange for food, cigarettes, and drugs. She had also reportedly engaged in sexual activities with her brother, Keith. To explain this early promiscuity, Wuornos claimed that she was sexually assaulted and beaten by her alcoholic grandfather. She claimed that prior to his frequent beatings, he forced her to remove her clothing. His alcoholism, coupled with his strictness, made both children incorrigible and rebellious.

At age 14, in 1970, Wuornos was raped by one of her grandfather's friends and became pregnant. She gave birth at a home for unwed mothers in January 1971, and her son was immediately placed for adoption after his birth. During her stay at the home, the staff described her as uncooperative and oftentimes hostile, unable to get along with her peers. A few months later, Wuornos dropped out of school. In July of the same year, her grandmother died of liver failure. Although Diane offered to let her children come live with her in Texas, they declined due to the expectation that they follow rules and maintain order while in her house. Thus, Wuornos and Keith became wards of the court.

When Wuornos was 15 years old, her grandfather threw her out of the house and she became a prostitute to support herself while living in the woods near her old home.

On 27 May 1974, Wuornos was arrested in Jefferson County, Colorado, for driving under the influence, disorderly conduct, and firing a .22-caliber gun from a moving vehicle. A failure-to-appear charge was later added.

Wuornos hitchhiked to Florida in 1976 where she met 69-year-old well-off yacht club president Lewis Gratz Fell who had a comfortable income from investing in railroad stocks. The odd couple was married that same year and their nuptials were printed in the local newspaper's society column. Due to her excessive drinking and subsequent confrontations at the local bar, she eventually went to jail for assault. She also struck Fell with his cane which led to his procurement of a restraining order against her. Consequently, she returned to Michigan.

On 14 July 1976, Wuornos was arrested in Antrim County, Michigan, for assault and disturbing the peace after throwing a cue ball at a bartender's head. This incident—in addition to Wuornos' habit of squandering his money and physically abusing him—provided the impetus for their split. After only nine weeks of marriage, on 21 July 1976, Wuornos and Fell annulled their marriage.

Wuornos' grandfather committed suicide soon thereafter and her brother Keith died of esophageal cancer on 17 July. Wuornos she received $10,000 from Keith's life insurance which she had wasted in only two months. She then went back to Florida and spent ten years in failed relationships and committing crimes, particularly prostitution; however, even as an "exit-to-exit interstate prostitute" she was "not a hot commodity" who was able to make enough money on which to live.

On 20 May 1981, Wuornos was, again, arrested for armed robbery; this time of an Edgewater, Florida, convenience store where she stole $35 and two packs of cigarettes. On 4 May 1982 she was sentenced to prison and was subsequently released on 30 June 1983. She was arrested again on 1 May 1984, in Key West for attempting to pass forged checks at a bank. On 30 November 1985, Wuornos was named as a suspect in the theft of a revolver and ammunition in Pasco County.

On 4 January 1986, Wuornos was arrested again in Miami for grand theft auto, resisting arrest, and obstruction of justice for attempting to provide her aunt's identification as her own. Police discovered a .38-caliber revolver and a box of ammunition inside the stolen vehicle.

On 2 June, Volusia County deputy sheriffs questioned Wuornos after a male companion accused her of pulling a gun on him in his car and demanding $200. At the time she had been carrying spare ammunition, and a .22-caliber pistol was found under the passenger seat in which she had occupied.

At about this same time, Wuornos met hotel maid Tyria Moore at a Daytona gay bar. Tired of her failed relationships with men, in addition to being lonely and angry, Wuornos was ready for something new. The women soon moved in together and Wuornos supported them both with her prostitution earnings. On 4 July 1987, Daytona Beach police detained the two women for questioning regarding an incident in which they were accused of assault and battery with a beer bottle.

On 12 March 1988, Wuornos—under the alias of Cammie Marsh Greene—accused a bus driver in Daytona Beach of assault; having claimed he pushed her off the bus following a confrontation. Moore was named as a witness. In November that same year, Wuornos—under another alias, Susan Blahovec—placed threatening phone calls over six days to a Zephyr Hills supermarket after an altercation over lottery tickets. Wuornos' demeanor continued to worsen, becoming wholly erratic and belligerent by 1989.

By the time Wuornos started killing, she had amassed a long rap sheet and had demonstrated a considerable history of violence, quick anger, hostility, rage, and a lack of conscience.

The Crimes

Richard Mallory, 51

Wuornos murdered 51-year-old Clearwater electronics shop owner Richard Mallory—who was a convicted rapist—on 30 November 1989. Mallory often closed his shop and disappeared for several days at a time on drinking and sex binges. He was not a great employer either, only having employees long enough to remove the backlog of work that accrued during his disappearances, only to fire them once his repair orders were caught up. When he failed to return to work in early December 1989, nobody really thought much of it.

On 1 December, a Volusia County deputy sheriff found an abandoned 1977 Cadillac just outside of Daytona Beach that was identified as belonging to Mallory.

On 13 December 1989, Jimmy Bonchi and James Davis were looking for scrap metal along a dirt road near Interstate 95 in Volusia County, Florida. Instead, they found a fully-clothed body wrapped in carpet.

Despite being badly decomposed, investigators were able to take the corpse's fingerprints which identified him as Richard Mallory. He had been shot three times in the chests with a .22-caliber pistol and the cause of death was attributed to two bullets in his left lung having hemorrhaged.

Several months of investigation into Mallory's "sordid lifestyle and somewhat shady acquaintances" did not provide detectives with any clues or potential suspects. Initially, a stripper who went by "Chastity" attracted suspicion; however, further investigation yielded little evidence with none of it attributable to "Chastity".

After several months, the case went cold.

Following her arrest, Wuornos would claim that she had shot Mallory in self-defense.

David Spears, 43

Heavy equipment operator and construction worker David Spears, 43, of Bradenton, Florida, was last seen on 19 May 1990.

His truck was discovered shortly thereafter on Interstate 75, unlocked and with the license plate missing.

Spears was later found, nude except for a baseball cap, on 1 June, along Highway 19 in Citrus County. Initially Spears was a John Doe; however, on 7 June he was identified as Spears. He had died of six bullet wounds to his torso.

Charles Carskaddon, 40

40-year-old part-time rodeo worker Charles Carskaddon was murdered by Wuornos on 31 May 1990.

His severely decomposed, nude body was found on 6 June, in Pasco County. Due to the extreme state of decomposition, medical examiners were neither able to obtain fingerprints nor could they estimate the corpse's time of death. Like Spears, initially, this victim became another John Doe, and lead Pasco County Detective Tom Muck could not immediately identify him. However, Muck had heard about the case in Citrus County and spoke to Citrus County Sheriff's Investigator Marvin Padgett about similarities present in both of their cases and the two men agreed to remain in touch.

During the autopsy, the medical examiner discovered nine small-caliber bullets throughout the victim's chest and abdomen.

Peter Siems, 65

65-year-old retired merchant seaman and Christian outreach ministry volunteer Peter Siems had left Jupiter, Florida, en route to Arkansas to visit relatives on 7 June 1990. Jupiter Police Detective John Wisnieski had been working on Siems' case since he was reported missing. Wisnieski distributed a nationwide message that contained descriptions of the two women, as well as a synopsis of the case and sketches of the two women to the Florida Criminal Activity Bulletin; however, the detective was not confident that he would find Siems alive.

One witness, Rhonda Bailey, was sitting on her porch when she saw Wuornos and her girlfriend Tyria Moore leaving Siems' car where it had landed following an accident in Orange Springs, on 4 July, when the car careened off State Road 315 and landed in some brush. Bailey watched as two women "clambered frantically from the car, throwing beer cans into the woods and swearing at each other." She told investigators that the brown-haired woman said little; however, the blonde—who had a bleeding arm injury—did the majority of the yelling. In fact, the blonde begged Bailey to not call the police, saying that her father lived just up the road.

The two women then got back into the significantly damaged car, but were only able to drive it a short distance. Ultimately, Wuornos and Moore abandoned it down the road and began walking. Orange Springs Volunteer Fireman Hubert Hewett responded to a call about the accident and asked the two women if they had been the ones in the car. Wuornos, cursing at him, said they had not and neither did they want any help. Hewett let them be and they continued to walk up the road.

Marion County Sheriff's Department deputies found the gray, four-door, 1988 Pontiac Sunbird where the women left it. The windshield and front door windows were smashed and there were bloodstains throughout the interior. The license plate was also missing. A computer check of the vehicle's VIN revealed Peter Siems as the owner.

A palm print on the interior door handle matched Wuornos'.

Siems' body has never been found.

Troy Burress, 50

50-year-old sausage salesman for Gilchrist Sausage in Ocala, Troy Burress was reported missing on 30 July by his manager, Johnny Mae

Thompson, after discovering that Burress had not shown up for his last few delivery stops. Later that night, she and her husband began looking for him. At 2:00 a.m., Burress' wife reported him missing and at 4:00 a.m. his truck was found by Marion County Sheriff's deputies on the shoulder of State Road 19, 20 miles east of Ocala. The car was unlocked, the keys were missing, and Burress was nowhere to be found.

He was found on 4 August, in a wooded area along State Road 19 in Marion County by a family picnicking in the Ocala National Forest; eight miles from where his truck was found.

Despite substantial decomposition courtesy of the Florida heat and humidity, Burress' wife was able to identify his wedding ring. During his autopsy it was determined that he had been shot twice with a .22-caliber gun; once in the head and once in the back.

Investigator John Tilley's initial suspect was a drifter named Curtis Michael Blankenship who had been hitchhiking along Highway 19 the day Burress disappeared and was picked up near the abandoned truck; however, as the investigation progressed, it became clear that Blankenship was not the murderer.

Unfortunately, Tilley had no more suspects at that time.

Charles "Dick" Humphreys, 56

Retired Air Force major, former police chief, and Florida state child abuse investigator Charles "Dick" Humphreys, 56, met his demise at Wuornos' hand on 11 September 1990. He had failed to return home from his last day of work at the Sumterville office of Florida's Department of Health and Rehabilitative Services where he specialized in investigating child abuse cases. He was planning on transferring to the Ocala office.

Humphreys had been married 35 years, having just celebrated his anniversary the previous day.

Humphreys' body was found in Marion County in the evening hours of 12 September. He was fully clothed and had been shot seven times; six bullets were found in his head and torso, while the seventh bullet went through his wrist and was never recovered.

His car was subsequently found in Suwannee County, Florida, toward the end of the month.

Walter Jeno Antonio, 62

62-year-old Walter Jeno Antonio—a police reservist—was Wuornos' last victim. His nude body was found on 19 November off of a remote logging road in Dixie County. He had been shot four times in the back and head with a .22 and it had been determined that he had been dead for less than 24 hours.

His vehicle was recovered five days later in Brevard County.

Investigation and Arrest

Captain Steve Binegar was in charge of the Marion County Sheriff's Criminal Investigation Division and was familiar with the Citrus and Pasco Counties cases. He could not ignore the similarities among those cases and the ones in his jurisdiction. Along with a multi-agency task force comprised of investigators from counties where victims were found, Binegar formulated a theory that the murderer(s) "had to be initially non-threatening to the victims"—namely women; particularly the two women who had wrecked Peter Siems' vehicle and left.

Binegar turned to the press for help in late November. Reuters ran a story about the murders stating the police were looking for the women. Florida papers picked up the article and published it along with the police sketches of Wuornos and Moore. Leads poured in almost immediately.

One man in Homosassa Springs said that two women who matched the sketches rented a trailer from him a year ago and identified them as Tyria Moore and Aileen Wuornos. Another woman in Tampa told police that the two women had worked at her motel and identified them as Tyria Moore and Susan Blahovec. Another caller identified the women as Tyria Moore and Lee Blahovec. However, the "mother lode" came from Port Orange where police had been tracking Lee Blahovec's and Tyria Moore's movements and were able to provide a detailed account of their actions from late September to mid-December. They stayed primarily at the Fairview Motel in Harbor Oaks where Blahovec registered as Cammie Marsh Greene. They also lived in a small apartment near the Fairview behind a restaurant. Police ran background checks and found that Moore had no record to speak of; however, Blahovec had one trespassing arrest and Greene had no record at all. Of particular interest was that the picture on Blahovec's license did not match Greene's.

Police also ran the fingerprints found on pawned items that belonged to the victims. In Daytona, they found that Cammie Marsh Greene had traded in a camera and radar detector that had belonged to Richard Mallory and had left a thumbprint on the receipt. And in Ormand Beach, Greene pawned a set of tools that belonged to David Spears. When the prints were run through the Automated Fingerprint Identification System (APHIS) in Volusia County, the report stated the prints belonged to Lori Grody who had a weapons charge and outstanding warrant. The bloody palm print found in Siems' car also matched Lory Grody's prints. When all of this information was sent to the National Crime Information Center (NCIC), police were informed that Lory Grady, Susan Blahovec, and Cammie Marsh Greene were all aliases for Aileen Carol Wuornos.

The official hunt for Wuornos began on 5 January 1991, and on 8 January, two undercover Georgia "drug dealers" named "Bucket" and "Drums" (who were, in fact, Mike Joyner and Dick Martin) saw her at the Port Orange Pub. While their "takedown" was planned to be gradual as they wanted an airtight case, Port Orange police officers entered suddenly and took Wuornos outside where Joyner phoned the command post at the Pirate's Cove Motel which was the command center for the multi-jurisdiction task force. Later, Bob Kelley of the

Volusia County Sheriff's Office called the Port Orange police station and told them not to arrest Wuornos under any circumstances.

Shortly thereafter, Wuornos returned to the bar and Joyner and Martin struck up a conversation with her and bought her beers. At approximately 10:00 p.m., she declined an offer for a ride from them and left. Again, the takedown was almost ruined when Florida Department of Law Enforcement officers followed Wuornos with their lights off as she walked down Ridgwood Avenue. Command pots officers put in a call and got the FDLE officers to leave so Wuornos could reach her next destination: a biker bar named the Last Resort. Joyner and Martin bought her more beers and engaged in more conversation. Shortly after midnight the two undercover officers left and Wuornos fell asleep on an old car seat at the bar.

The next afternoon, 9 January, Joyner and Martin returned to the Last Resort, "talking Wuornos up and wearing transmitters that kept the police apprised of everything that went on." Despite having planned to arrest her the night before, the decision was made at the command post to arrest her that afternoon. Joyner and Martin asked Wuornos if she wanted to clean up at their motel room. She accepted and left the bar with the two men.

Outside, Marion County Sheriff's Office Detective Larry Horzepa approached Wuornos and informed her she was under arrest for the outstanding warrant under Lori Grody's name. No mention of the murders was made, nor was any announcement given to media that the murder suspect had been apprehended.

The following day, police found Moore in Pittston, Pennsylvania, living with her sister. Jerry Thompson of Citrus County and Bruce Munster of Marion flew to Scranton to interview Moore. Moore told them that she had known about the murders since Wuornos had come home with Mallory's Cadillac and openly confessed that she had killed a man that day. Moore told Wuornos not to say anything else. This occurred whenever Wuornos came home with different items; Moore told her she didn't want to hear it because the more she knew, the more compelled she might have felt to report Wuornos to the police and she was scared of her even though Wuornos told her she would never hurt her.

On the flight home, Thompson and Munster persuaded Moore to elicit a confession from Wuornos in exchange for prosecutorial immunity. They wanted an airtight case and a confession would make it so. Moore returned to Florida with the police and was put up in a motel. With police guidance, Moore made several telephone calls to Wuornos in which she told her that the police had been questioning her family and that she was afraid that the murders might be pinned on her. Moore asked Wuornos for help in clearing her name. All of these calls were recorded. On 16 January 1991, Wuornos provided a shocking and detailed confession to the murders; however, she claimed that she had killed them all in self-defense after they tried to rape her. Wuornos repeatedly asserted that Moore had absolutely nothing to do with the murders and that she would ensure that Moore would not go to jail.

Many found it hard to believe that every single one of Wuornos' victims actually tried to rape her, particularly since she made a living as a prostitute. She was known for exaggeration—such as her claim that she had "serviced" as many as 250,000 johns. In fact, in order to make that allegation true, Wuornos would have had to have slept with 35 different men each day for 20 years.

With all of the media attention focused upon her, Wuornos felt famous and continued to talk herself up about the crimes to anyone who would listen, even Volusia County Jail staff. Each subsequent retelling of her story portrayed her in a better light.

Trials and Convictions

During her trial, Wuornos was legally adopted by a well-meaning, born-again Christian, horse breeder named Arlen Pralle who was 44 at the time, and her husband. Pralle claimed that she was following God's instructions and added that she and Wuornos don't talk about the case during their weekly visits and nightly telephone calls. She said that in her heart she knew that Wuornos was not a serial killer but had a "heart of gold", "cares about other people more than herself", and that God had brought them together.

Originally, Wuornos' attorneys created a plea bargain—to which she agreed—wherein she would plead guilty to six charges in exchange for six consecutive life sentences; however, one state attorney thought she should receive the death penalty and on 14 January 1992, she went on trial for the murder of Richard Mallory. Whereas prior bad acts are typically inadmissible in criminal trials, Florida's Williams Rule permits prosecutors to introduce evidence of other crimes to demonstrate a pattern of deviant activity which the prosecution did with the other murders. This was exceedingly inculpatory because had the jury known only of Mallory's past then it could have fathomed that she did, in fact, kill him in self-defense; however, by having knowledge of the other murders, the jury easily discounted her self-defense defense.

Over her public defenders' protestations, Wuornos insisted upon taking the stand to tell her own story. As the jury had already heard her taped confession, her account of Mallory's murder she gave in court was dramatically different. She testified that Mallory raped, sodomized, and tortured her; however, on cross-examination, prosecutor John Tanner destroyed any shred of credibility she might have had remaining. When her inconsistencies and lies were highlighted, Wuornos—as was her nature—became visibly angry. Wuornos then invoked her Fifth Amendment right against self-incrimination 25 times.

Wuornos was found guilty of first-degree murder on 27 January 1992. At her sentencing hearing, defense psychiatrists proffered testimony that Wuornos was mentally unstable and suffered from both borderline and antisocial personality disorders; however, jurors unanimously recommended that she receive the death penalty. Four days later, Judge Uriel Blount sentenced her to just that.

On 31 March 1992, Wuornos pled no contest to the murders of Dick Humphreys, Troy Burress, and David Spears. She had stated that she wanted to "get right with God" and, subsequently, provided a statement to the court in which she said, "I wanted to confess to you that Richard Mallory did violently rape me as I've told you; but these others did not. [They] only began to start to."

On 15 May of that same year, Wuornos was given three more death sentences.

Wuornos later plead guilty to the murder of Charles Carskaddon in June 1992 and in November was given her fifth death sentence despite defense efforts to introduce evidence that Mallory had been tried for intent to commit rape in Maryland and, in fact, had been incarcerated in a maximum-security correctional facility that provided treatment to sexual offenders. In fact, records obtained from that facility demonstrated that between 1958 and 1962 Mallory had, in fact, served time there stemming from a criminal attempted rape charge and received eight years of "treatment". However, the judge refused to admit this evidence at trial and denied Wuornos' request for a retrial.

Then, in February 1993, Wuornos pled guilty to Walter Antonio's murder and was given yet another death sentence.

As Peter Siems' body was never found, Wuornos was not charged in his murder.

When all was said and done, Wuornos received six death sentences for first-degree murder.

During her trials, she related several inconsistent stories. Initially, Wuornos claimed that all seven of her victims had raped her; however, she later recanted her self-defense claim except against Mallory. During one interview with filmmaker Nick Broomfield who produced two documentaries about her life, Wuornos had told him—when she thought the cameras were off—that her murders were, in fact, self-defense; however, she could not stand being on death row and wanted to die. At this point she had been on death row for 12 years and appealing her cases would have likely taken decades more.

After her initial appeal to the United States Supreme Court was denied n 1996, Wuornos decided, in 2001, that she would not pursue any further appeals regarding her death sentences. She petitioned the Florida Supreme Court for the right to fire her attorney and cease all appeals. She stated:

"I killed those men, robbed them as cold as ice. And I'd do it again, too. There's no chance in keeping me alive or anything, because I'd kill again. I have hate crawling through my system ... I am so sick of hearing this 'she's crazy' stuff. I've been evaluated so many times. I'm competent, sane, and I'm trying to tell the truth. I'm one who seriously hates human life and would kill again." Despite her statements appearing to be given rationally, her defense attorney argued that she was in no state for the court to honor her request.

In response, then-governor Jeb Bush had a trio of psychiatrists evaluate Wuornos' competency to be executed. In the state of Florida, such a test requires that the evaluators be "convinced that the condemned person understands that she will die and for which crime(s) she is being executed." All three psychiatrists determined that she was, in fact, mentally fit to be executed.

Despite being assessed as competent, Wuornos later started accusing prison staffs of abusing her: spitting on her food, serving her potatoes cooked in dirt, dousing her food in urine. She also claimed that she overhead conversations where individuals allegedly stated that they were trying to get her "so pushed over the brink by them" that she would end up committing suicide before her execution. Additionally, Wuornos complained of frequent strip searches, of being handcuffed so tightly that her wrists were bruised any time she left her cell, of door kicking and frequent window checks by staff, of low water pressure, of mildew in her cell and on her mattress, of cat calling, and of overhearing conversations where conspiracies to rape her were planned. She subsequently threatened to boycott food and showers when certain staff was on duty. Her attorney asserted that his client simply wanted proper, humane treatment until the day she is executed and that even if her allegations proved to be figments of her imagination, she clearly believed them.

Prior to her execution, Wuornos granted an interview to Broomfield wherein she claimed that her mind was "being controlled by 'sonic pressure' to make her appear crazy" as well as describing her impending death "as being taken away by angels on a space ship." She told Broomfield, "You sabotaged my ass, society, and the cops, and the system. A raped woman got executed, and was used for books and movies and shit." After her execution, Broomfield spoke to one of Wuornos' childhood friends, Dawn Botkins, who told him that Wuornos' statements were not meant as a personal affront to him but toward the media in general, as well as the criminal justice system.

Execution

Wuornos' last meal consisted of $20 worth of Kentucky Fried Chicken and a cup of coffee.

She was taken into the death chamber at Florida State Prison near Starke on 9 October 2002, and was strapped upon the gurney where lethal drugs were pumped into her arms at 9:30 a.m. Eastern Daylight Time. At 9:31 a.m. she closed her eyes as her head jerked backward. One minute later her mouth dropped open and her eyes narrowed to slits. She was pronounced dead at 9:47 a.m.

Her final words were, "Yes, I would just like to say I'm sailing with the rock, and I'll be back, like Independence Day with Jesus. June 6, like the movie. Big mother ship and all, I'll be back, I'll be back."

Wuornos was the tenth woman in the United States to be executed since the United States Supreme Court lifted the ban on the death penalty in 1976 pursuant to *Gregg v. Georgia*, and the second woman ever executed in the state of Florida between 1976 and October 2002;

the first being Judy Buenoano who was convicted for the 1971 murder of her husband James Goodyear, the 1980 murder of her son Michael Buenoano, and the 1983 attempted murder of fiancé John Gentry.

Wuornos' body was cremated and taken by her friend Botkins to Michigan who spread her ashes beneath a tree. She requested that Natalie Merchant's song "Carnival" be played at her funeral and, in fact, Merchant commented on this when questioned as to why her song was played during the credits of the documentary *Aileen: Life and Death of a Serial Killer*. Merchant stated that despite being "so disturbed" about the subject matter of the documentary that she could not even bring herself to watch it, when she found out that Wuornos often listened to her album *Tigerlily* while on death row and requested that "Carnival" be played at her funeral that she gave permission. Merchant said, "it's very odd to think of the places my music can go once it leaves my hands. If it gave her some solace, I have to be grateful."

Her victims' family members are not sorry that she was executed. Some have commented that she got off quite easily both while on death row and during her execution, while her victims and their families suffered tremendously.

Volusia County State Attorney John Tanner—who prosecuted Wuornos—felt obligated to attend her execution and commented that Wuornos liked to be in control. The murders were, simply, exacting the ultimate control over someone by terminating his life.

Aftermath

Wuornos' life has been immortalized in film. In the 1992 television movie *Overkill: The Aileen Wuornos Story*, Wuornos was portrayed by Jean Smart. The theatrical film *Monster* (2003) that chronicled Wuornos' life from childhood until her first murder conviction starred Charlize Theron who won a Best Actress Academy Award for her portrayal of Wuornos.

As for books, Sue Russell's *Lethal Intent* (2002) is about Wuornos. Additionally, Lisa Kester and Daphne Gottlieb edited and published a collection of letters Wuornos had written to her childhood friend Dawn Botkins over a ten-year period entitled *Dear Dawn: Aileen Wuornos in Her Own Words* (2012).

Famed FBI profiler Robert K. Ressler, who famously coined the term "serial killer", mentioned Wuornos—albeit briefly—in his autobiography of his 20 years with the FBI. In his 1992 book *Whoever Fights Monsters* he stated that while he typically does not discuss female serial killers because instead of being "true" serial killers they "tend to kill in sprees instead of in a sequential fashion", he noted that Wuornos was the sole exception and was a true serial killer in that she was a murderer who sought personal gratification instead of financial gain as was often the case for women who had murdered spouses or lodgers, or even those females who murdered while under the influence of postpartum psychosis.

Additionally, Rima Banerji's poem "Sugar Zero" is also dedicated to Wuornos and appears in the 2005 Arsenal Pulp Press publication, *Red Light: Superheroes, Saints, and Sluts*.

Filmmaker Nick Broomfield directed two documentaries about Wuornos: *Aileen Wuornos: The Selling of a Serial Killer* (1993) and *Aileen: Life and Death of a Serial Killer* (2003). Broomfield speculated that Wuornos' anger was deep-seated and while working as a prostitute she likely had many "awful encounters" on the roads which forced said anger to explode from her into incredible violence just so she could survive. He also stated he believes that Wuornos believed that she, in fact, had killed in self-defense and that her psychosis skewed her behavior between one who exhibited immense rages and another with incredible humanity inside of her.

The documentary television series *American Justice, Biography, and Deadly Women* featured Wuornos in several episodes and she was in an episode of *The New Detectives* entitled "Fatal Compulsion" that aired in season three (episode one).

On 22 June 2001, San Francisco's Yerba Buena Center for the Arts premiered an operatic adaptation of Wuornos' life entitled *Wuornos* that was written by Carla Lucero, conducted by Mary Chun, and produced by the Jon Sims Center for the Performing Arts. Additionally, several songs have been written about Wuornos including Jewel's "Nicotine Love" and the New York metalcore band It Dies Today's "Sixth of June." Singer Diamanda Galás recorded a live cover of the Phil Ochs song "Iron Lady" on her performance album *Malediction and Prayer* as a tribute to Wuornos.

Finally, the hit television show *American Horror* Story, in its fifth season's *Hotel* had Lily Rabe portraying a fictionalized version of Wuornos as part of a Halloween storyline and again in the season finale.

SHE DEVIL: THE TRUE STORY OF MYRA HINDLEY

ELLEN THOMAS

In the early 1960s, Myra Hindley took her first job out of school at a small chemical company called Millwards Merchandise. A shy eighteen-year-old, she kept to herself, reading in the office courtyard during breaks.

But she only did this to attract her co-worker, Ian Brady.

Brady would spend his breaks reading books. Myra soon followed suit in the hopes that he would approach.

After several months, the Glasgow, Scotland native finally made his move.

They both worked at the office as clerks. Brady was four years older than her as they began to date.

Myra lived with her grandmother and gave her virginity to the awkward co-worker on her grandmother's sofa. She would soon become Brady's accomplice in some of the most gruesome child killings in the history of Great Britain.

A BAD NEWS CHARACTER

Brady already had a police record for petty theft. He also had a strange demeanor, tilting his head oddly at people as he stared them down with hooded eyes.

He was nicknamed "Lassie", not a reference to the Collie dog but to his feminine body language. Brady was tall, skinny and would indicate later that he was a bisexual. As a child, he had few friends and was called "Dracula" in the neighborhood. He would torture kittens and see how long it took for them to die.

They were both bookworms and Brady would give Myra books on the Marquis De Sade, trying to introduce her to the world of sexual sadism. After their dates, he would invite her back to his place and play back recordings of Adolph Hitler's speeches.

The young couple would come up with pet nicknames for each other. Myra would call Ian "Hetty" after a character in the Goons and he would call her "Hess" after Hitler's deputy. They would soon become inseparable, both strangely odd people that felt that were superior and set apart from everyone else.

It soon became clear, however, that Ian was influencing Myra and not the other way around. He was her guide to the world of sexual sadism and then later, slowly revealed his desire to rape and murder children.

He started this by sharing a book in the same way he introduced her to sadomasochism. The book had detailed the "crime of the century". A child was the victim and one of the characters was named Myra.

"He had given me a book called 'Compulsion,'" Myra recalled. "Which was the story of Leopold and Loeb. They decided to commit the perfect murder. They were studying the philosophy of Nietzsche, his theory of the superiority of the pure Aryan and the strong overcoming the weak. It was very much the Nazi philosophy. They kidnapped a twelve-year-old boy for a ransom. They killed him, were caught and sent to prison. I told him it was a very disturbing book. But why exactly had he wanted me to read it? He told me he wanted to do a perfect murder and I was going to help him. That was why he needed me to pick someone up as I was a woman and a child would be more trusting of a woman. I burst into tears and he slapped my head backward and forward. I managed to fight him off and told him to stop it."

Myra fell prey to Ian's system of push and pull psychology. He would be abusive to Myra then inexplicably turn around and be sweet to her.

"I must be totally honest and say he wasn't always cruel and sadistic towards me," Myra said. "We had some pleasant times in country places that he'd found during his travels on his bike. We'd pack a picnic lunch, lots of coffee, bottles of wine and spend whole days in peace and tranquility. That was such a contrast to the other side of him. These were moments I treasured and thought about when things were bad. Trying to remember, telling myself that he couldn't help what he was and maybe in time he would become accustomed to ordinary domesticity and we could live a normal life."

IDLE HANDS

"Myra was a bored English girl looking for some adventure," forensic psychologist Paula Orange said. "Brady had an edge about him. Myra liked that about him, she wanted out of her dull life and into a world of edgy darkness, if you will."

Myra didn't judge Brady for being an avowed Nazi. She thought he was just going through a phase but he continued to play Richard Wagner's music full blast and storm around the house dressed up in Nazi regalia. Working himself up into a frenzy, he would then play rough sex games with Myra.

Myra found this aspect of Brady's personality to be alluring. She enjoyed dressing up in leather and black stockings, indulging whatever fantasy Brady could come up with.

"She was a sheltered young woman," Orange said. "And Brady opened up a whole new world to her. Think of it as 'Fifty Shades of Grey' with some Nazism thrown in and you have the whole relationship of Myra Hindley and Ian Brady."

The kinky sex continued and Brady gave stronger indications that he wanted to commit the perfect murder.

He wanted to harm children.

But he needed an accomplice.

"We can make the case that Myra made the jump from sadomasochistic sex to murder out of an obligation to Ian," Orange said. "It gave her a rush, to follow his lead. She needed more and more to get that same high."

The two would feed off each other sexually after which Ian would begin to plot the murders out. Who would be their victim? How would they kill them? Where would they kill them? He wrote things out in advance to the most minute detail.

"She (Myra) became desperate to fulfill his fantasies, his needs," journalist Clint Entwhistle said. "She was frightened, I suspect, of rejection by him."

So Myra didn't report him. She went along with his program.

SNAPPED

Brady had made his decision that they were going to kill someone. The night before, he took Myra to a bar on the back of his motorcycle. The two parked a little beyond the pub itself. Ian then began to intimidate Myra. He was jealous that she took a ride home from a co-worker.

"All the time we were talking," Myra recalled. "He was running a knife across his fingers. I honestly thought he was going to stab me. Then he laughed, put the knife away, told me never to accept a lift (the co-worker) again, and we drove back to the pub."

"Later as we were driving home, I dreaded what he would do when we got there, for I knew he would do something. "He raped me anally, urinated inside me and, whilst doing so, began strangling me until I nearly passed out. Then he bit me on the cheekbone, just below my right eye, until my face began to bleed. I tried to fight him off strangling me and biting me, but the more I did, the more the pressure increased. Before he left, when he'd seen the state of my face, he told me to stay off work the next day ..."

This would all take place under the roof of Myra's grandmother who was asleep when the assault took place.

"My gran almost fainted when she saw me and went to get my mother, who asked me if ' He' had done that to me. My mother disliked him intensely and kept telling me he was no good for me; she'd been telling me that since I'd met him at 18 and a half, but what girl of that age listens to her mother when she is wholly infatuated and in love? I told them what he had told me to say (she had been hit by a beer bottle during a bar fight) but I knew they didn't believe me."

THE FIRST MURDER

The following night after he beat down Myra, Brady selected his first victim.

He spotted a teenage girl walking to a dance by herself. She wore a sky blue jacket over a button-down red polka dot dress. Her white gloves and high heels turned on Ian Brady but what really arrested his attention was her face.

Cute with an air of innocence. A face that had an easy vulnerability, someone who would crack under the pressure of his whip.

Her pain and tears would be delicious, Ian thought.

Her name was Pauline Reede.

Brady gave Ian her orders and told her to pick the girl up. He would follow them on his bike.

"Ian Brady was awkward," Entwistle said. "He was not the kind of person a child would trust. There is no way anyone would have gotten into a car with him."

That is what he needed Myra for.

Myra did as he said, driving up alongside Pauline as she walked on the deserted road. The two young woman had already known each other from around the neighborhood.

"Can I give you a lift?" Myra asked.

"Oh, thank you, sure," Polly got into the small white van.

"Where are you going?"

"To the dance hall-"

"Okay," Myra said. "I just have to go to the Moors. I just lost one of my gloves. You can help me look for it. It will only take a second."

Pauline simply nodded her head. She trusted Myra.

THE KILLING FIELDS

"The Moors above Manchester were a special place for Ian Brady and Myra Hindley," Entwistle said. "They picnicked there together. They'd have sex there. It was a very, very important place to them."

It would also be the place where they would commit their first murder together.

Myra stepped off the van and directed Polly to look through some bushes. It was dark and Pauline asked if they should just look for it in the morning. Myra laughed it off and walked away, feigning as if she were looking for her gloves.

Ian Brady waited in the bushes, his mouth dry with anticipation, as he watched the sixteen-year-old Polly sift through the bushes.

Sneaking behind his victim, he slammed her across the head with a shovel.

Pauline Reede fell to the ground, stunned.

She would then be raped, tortured then murdered by the sadistic Brady.

"Brady was a sadist," Orange said. "He got off on the suffering of his young victim. The more innocent she was, the more she screamed, the more she pleaded for her life, the more he got off. It was part of the high for him. He had moved beyond the bedroom thrills with Myra and needed a bigger high. He wanted his fantasy to become reality."

Brady assaulted Pauline until she lost consciousness.

No longer able to provide him the "fun" of listening to her suffer, he took a knife to her throat and killed her.

Myra watched in silence as Ian Brady commit the brutal crime and then proceeded to bury Polly in a shallow grave.

"He led me to her body which I tried not to look at," Myra wrote. "I didn't know at the time that he was testing me at there was no need for me to be there. He told me to look at here. I'll never be able to forget what I saw. I stood and looked at the dark outline of the rocks against the horizon of the dark sky. Three people died that night. Pauline. My soul. And God. No God would have let what had happened, happen."

On the surface, however, Myra didn't seem distressed about the murder. She went to work the following Monday as if nothing happened.

"You would think if she had any conscience left she would have gone to the authorities," Orange said. "But Myra had been dehumanized by that point. The daily rapes and assaults made her numb to everything."

Still, a part of her old self remained. The disappearance of Pauline Reade sent shockwaves throughout Manchester. Myra was reading the newspaper one day and noticed a personal column written by Pauline Reade's mother.

It read " Pauline, please come home. We're heartbroken for you."

"I began to cry," Myra recalled. "Rocking myself back and forth with the paper clutched to my chest. I didn't hear his bike, nor knew that he'd come into the house. He asked me what was wrong but I couldn't answer; I couldn't stop shaking and crying, for I was devastated about what had happened to Pauline, and for her mum and dad. I really liked Mrs. Reade and used to feel sorry for her because she had problems with her nerves and always looked as though she was on the edge of a breakdown. He grabbed the paper off me and soon saw what I'd seen."

"He put the bolt on the front door in case gran came back, did the same to the back door, and began to strangle me. Before I lost consciousness, I heard him remind me of what he'd said after Pauline's murder, and that threat still stood. After the first murder, as we were driving home, he told me that if I'd shown any signs of backing out, I would have finished up in the same grave as Pauline."

MYRA'S EARLY LIFE

As one would expect, Myra grew up in an abusive home.

Her parents engaged in daily shouting matches which she watched from behind her bedroom door.

Her father would routinely beat her mother, exposing Myra to sudden violence during her formative years. He was a competitive boxer who would also engage in weekend bar brawls.

"He used to beat her a lot," Entwhistle said. "Her father was a very, very powerful influence on her life. She had a tough personality type to start with. If you combine that with a violent childhood, a childhood where she was taught how to be violent, how to be aggressive, then you end up with an unusual personality type."

Myra hated her father and saw him as a bully. He would teach her to box, often hitting her across the head when she performed the techniques incorrectly.

"My father wielded total parental control," Myra said. "I rebelled against it. Fought against it. All my life until I was old enough to free myself from it. All his attempts to control me, even the successful ones were at great cost and were the result of bitter recriminations and often a hard physical punishment."

Myra's father would give her spankings without warning, leaving her buttocks bruised.

Once when she was bullied by a little boy and came home with bruises on her face, her father locked her out of the house. He told her to either face down the bully or he was going to beat her up himself.

"I set up the street to meet my persecutor," Myra recalled. "I quickly concentrated on whatDad had told me and showed me. As Kenny's hand came up, I shot up my left hand, fist bunched towards his head. As I predicted, both hands went up to protect his face and I lifted my right hand and slammed it into his tummy, hitting him hard. With a gasp, Kenny Holden's knees crumbled and before he could recover I slammed my left fist into the side of his head. Kenny was so heavily shocked he sat down heavily on the floor and burst into tears. I stood looking down at him triumphantly."

Myra saw a lot of her father in Ian Brady. Aggressive. Ultra-violent.

"Myra did what we call in psychology, 'transference,'" Orange said. "She saw in Ian what she saw in her father. She never got her daddy's love. So in her mind, she saw Ian as Daddy. She wanted Daddy's love and would do whatever Ian wanted. That was part of her cycle. Transferring a deep need for her father's love onto Ian. There is the strong possibility that had Myra never hooked up with Ian she would have never become a murderer. But the two of them together? Horrific results."

"The bringing together of Myra Hindley and Ian Brady," Entwhistle said. "Unleashed an appalling set of criminal acts."

POLLY IS STILL MISSING

The disappearance of Polly Reede sent the town of Manchester on edge. Things like that simply didn't happen there.

"The fact that children were being abducted and killed," Entwhistle said. "Was incomprehensible to the ordinary man and woman in the street."

Myra would soon find out that Ian's sexual fantasies were not limited to teenaged girls.

He wanted boys too.

Myra would again be a willing accomplice in procuring Ian's second victim. This time, it would be twelve-year-old John Killbride. Myra would befriend the young boy before bringing him to the Moors where he would be sexually assaulted by Brady and later killed.

"I had a terrible feeling something had happened to him," John Killbridge's mother recalled when her son didn't come home from school. "Because he wasn't the kind of boy who would leave home for any reason. He was quite happy and very pleasant, always singing and whistling and I just couldn't see him going anywhere with anyone. Unless it was in an innocent way, somebody wanting to do a job with him or something like that. He'd be enticed into a car that way."

Ian would take photos of the body and burial site. This would become part of their ritual, their ceremony. They would perform the murder then take photographs as if to mark the moment. Then they would return to the scene of the crime days after with their dog "Puppet" in tow. They would take more pictures and relive what took place only days earlier.

"He stopped me as I was walking (to take a picture)," Myra recalled. "And said to turnaround. Moved me about a bit. Told me to kneel down and look at 'Puppet' whose head was showing when he was still wrapped inside my coat. I now know, and knew quite soon afterward, that he photographed me virtually kneeling on John Killbride's grave."

AN INSATIABLE HUNGER

Four months had elapsed between the Pauline and John Killbride murders. But now Ian could not wait long. He ordered Myra to deliver another victim to the isolated Moors.

His name was Keith Bennett. An exuberant, trusting boy, Keith looked like the proverbial nerd with a gap-toothed smile and professorial eyeglasses.

"Keith was a cheeky little lad," Entwhistle said. "He liked to go out and have fun."

Trusting that Myra was taking him some place fun, the young Keith was ambushed by Brady who wrapped a cord around his neck.

Myra did her usual best to remain detached while the horrific attack took place.

"I hadn't wanted this to happen," Myra recalled. "I was tense and terrified. I tried to concentrate my mind miles away from where I was. Finally, after roughly what I think was a half an hour by which time dusk began to descend. I heard him whistle or call. When I stood up, he was waving me back down to the stream bed. Virtually nothing was said as we made our way back except for him saying the spade was hampering him and he'd have to hide it, which he did."

The twelve-year-old Keith, whose entire family was waiting for him at his grandmother's house, never showed up.

His entire family would be traumatized for life.

"I am a mother," Keith's mother, Winnie Johnson said. "It was my first lad and I've got to find him no matter what."

Keith Bennett's body was never found.

"I have nightmares," Johnson said. "I jump in my sleep. It's getting to me now. Because I just can't get him back."

Meanwhile, Myra and Ian would once again take mementos of their time together, taking photos of themselves along the Moors on Keith's fresh grave. Days later, the two would go to St. James Church for midnight mass.

"I retained a warm religious glow," Myra said. "And came out feeling warmed. Not so Ian who took a long swill of whiskey and went to the grave where he casually urinated."

RITUALS

The photos of their time together became an obsession for Ian Brady. He had an automatic camera where he would set the timer and pose for photographs with Myra. In a few of them, they would pose on top of the fresh graves with Ian playfully choking Myra.

"Myra and Ian would often return to the scenes of their crimes," Orange said. "They would take photos of themselves there and relive the thrill of committing the murders."

Over time, however, the photos would not be enough stimulation. They needed something better. Something more visceral.

Sounds.

Ian Brady decided he would record the audio of their next victim being tortured.

That next victim would be ten-year-old Leslie Ann Downey. Myra would befriend and abduct her from the county fairgrounds.

"They would take her back to their home," Entwistle said. "Where he photographed her and recorded her being tortured."

Ian Brady would listen to the audio tape over and over again, closing his eyes and remembering the horrific acts he committed.

Is is the murder of Leslie that Myra would refuse to talk about in interviews.

"There's a tape that isn't what people think it is," Myra said, trying to downplay her own sadism evident in the tapes. "But it's bad. I just hurt so much to think that I've been such a cruel bastard."

THE RUSH OF KILLING

Like a drug addict needing a bigger hit to get high, Brady needed more and more of a thrill for his next murder. He started to get sloppy whereas before his attacks were meticulously planned out.

His next victim would be Edward Evans.

"Edwards was sixteen, seventeen years old," Entwhistle said. "And he picked him up in a pub in Manchester."

This would be the first time Ian acted in tandem with Myra to obtain the victim. They enticed the young man to come over to their home and there were witnesses in the pub.

The couple also invited Myra's brother in law, Dave Smith to watch the carnage.

"Smith had no idea what was going on," Entwhistle said. "He walked into it totally cold, totally unaware and soon found out that he was involved in the most horrific scene with blood all over the place. A man's head being smashed in."

Smith was appalled, then called the police and told them of the killing.

Police arrived on scene within minutes. They discovered the mauled body of Edwards in a tub. Both Ian and Myra would be arrested.

"It is inexplicable as to why the couple would allow Dave Smith to witness the murder," Orange said. "A part of me thinks that it was part of increasing the thrill. The desire to share what they felt was a special moment with someone else."

A CHILLING DISCOVERY

Investigators would then scour the home, finding one unusual clue that would reveal the goings on of the couple now known in the papers as the Moors Murderers.

They found a left over luggage ticket.

The police would go to the central train station and matched the ticket with a suitcase. Inside, the found something they would never forget.

"They kept trophies in suitcases," Entwhistle said. "In there, of course, was the tape recording of Leslie Ann Downey and that proved what they'd done."

The police would play back the tapes. It churned their stomach to hear the tearful cries of Leslie Ann Downey plead for her life.

"You need to do what he says," Hindley screamed at the little girl. "I told you to shut your face!"

"I want to go home," the little girl pleaded.

"Quiet! Do you not speak English?"

The tape would be played for the jurors at the trial of the couple.

According to witnesses, you could hear a pin drop when they played the tape in court.

"Afterward there was a long, stony silence," Entwhistle said. "As people reflected on what they just heard."

DENIAL

Myra would maintain her own innocence of the murders and repeatedly state that she never witnessed any of the killings herself.

"My solicitor (defense attorney) told me they'd found the body of a child," Myra said. "Identified as Lesley Ann Downey, did I know anything about it? And I said 'No.' A week after that, I'm not sure, they found John Killbride's body and they charged me with, I think it was the murder of John Killbride. Yes, it was. They set me down behind a table and behind it was a large poster of John Killbride. 'Will you just identify these pictures or these photos and tell us if you seen them before.' I'd say, yes, and then they turned over the picture to another photo of the unearthed body of John Killbride."

The picture, Myra would state, made her cry.

LETTERS TO MOMMA

Myra would write her mother numerous letters before her trial. She would order her mother to destroy the letters after she read them but her mother thought otherwise. She would also tell her mother to keep the photographs of her and Ian to herself.

"Don't believe what they're saying about us," Myra wrote. "It is all lies."

But the mothers of all the victims didn't see it that way.

In court, they all had an opportunity to confront Myra.

"The worst part was being confronted by Mrs. West in the witness box," Myra recalled. "And I was looking at her as she was giving evidence and she saw me looking at her and she screamed across at me. 'How can you look at me?' And she called me every name under the sun."

It is at this point that Myra stated that she began to fully realize the gravity of her crimes.

"It suddenly hit me just what I'd done and I think he (Ian) sensed this," Myra said. "We were sitting next to each other and he just put his hand on my arm and squeezed my arm. And I turned around and looked at him, and he was telling me with his eyes to keep quiet."

The jury would find them guilty and in May of 1966 both would be sentenced to life in prison.

STANDING BY HER MAN

Myra refused to testify against Ian. There were some legal experts at the time who believed that if she gave evidence against Brady she would have walked free. But she didn't. She elected to take the punishment along with him.

Instead, she accepted her sentencing and continued to write her mother.

"Dear Mum," Myra wrote. "I knew that I would have to go to prison for some time for 'harboring'. But I didn't think it would be for this long. Ian is in prison, in the special wing. Poor thing, he sews mailbags during the day. He says it helps to pass the time quicker than expected. Will you do one thing for me, ma'am? Take out a policy on me or for me, for a half gram a week. I can't even begin to think of the future. It will be something to fall back on."

"Ian has got a little mouse in his cell. He feeds it crumbs and sits in bed watching it nibble them. The other night, he left it half a chip, thinking it wouldn't touch it but when he woke up the next morning it had disappeared."

Over the next three years, Myra would bombard her mother with requests for the photographs of her and Ian together. She said she did this at the behest of Ian who wanted both the slides and photographs desperately. Myra's mother eventually relented by was sure to allow the police copies of the negatives.

"Ian wanted those pictures back so bad because it reminded him of the events," Orange said. "That is the sort of thing we've come to expect from certain types of serial killers. They want to relive the moment in their fantasy. They'll take mementos, pictures, different elements of their crime in order so they can relive it in their minds. The pictures of Myra holding their dog on those burial sites were of paramount importance to Ian."

Myra would die in prison in 2002 of respiratory failure. Her ashes would be scattered over the Moors, a place that she loved so much.

"Was Myra Hindley sick or was she evil?" Entwhistle asked. "She had a violent father. She met a sexually sadistic man who desperately wanted to be a serial killer. All those things came together and made her carry out some evil, appalling crimes."

Ian Brady remains alive, living out his years under suicide watch in a psychiatric facility where he has repeatedly stated that he will kill himself if given the chance.

bonus story:

Christa Gail Pike, born 10 March 1976, currently sits on Tennessee's death row for the murder of Colleen Slemmer, 19, on 12 January 1995. The murder occurred when Pike was 18 years old. Pike and her then-boyfriend Tadaryl Shipp who was 17 at the time of the murder were convicted of Slemmer's murder and conspiracy to commit murder. Another friend of the defendants and the victim, Shadolla Peterson, also 18 at the time, was convicted as an accessory after the fact and given six years' probation after turning informant. Pike was sentenced to death by electrocution in 1996 and, at the time, she had the distinction of being the youngest woman ever to be sentenced to death, in any state and only the second women given the death penalty in Tennessee.

Early Life

Pike's life reads like a primer for depraved murderers. As a small child, Pike did not enjoy a healthy and supportive bond with her mother, Carissa Hansen, a licensed nurse, allegedly because of her premature birth. Whereas thousands of children are born prematurely and do not resort to criminal behavior Pike's birth was presented as evidence of one possible origin of her poor and troubled behavior. Pike's maternal grandmother was verbally abusive and Pike was raised by her alcoholic and abusive paternal grandmother until the latter's death in 1988 when Pike was 12; after which Pike attempted suicide by overdosing. She was then shuttled back and forth between her divorced parents' homes. In 1989, Pike was kicked out of her father's house for the second and final time due to her unruliness and the alleged sexual abuse of her father's then-two-year old daughter with his second wife.

Prior to the murder, experts assert that there were myriad indications that Pike was seriously disturbed; however, nobody who may have suspected this sought help for the increasingly disobedient and incorrigible young lady. According to Pike's mother, she was problematic since the age of eight and the two of them had a contentious relationship due to Pike's fluctuating and troubling behavior. Her mother asserted that by age nine Pike was growing marijuana in pots at their home and had been permitted to have a live-in boyfriend at age 14. At one point—in an effort to improve their relationship—Hansen suggested that she and Pike smoke marijuana together. Hansen mistakenly believed that cultivating a friendship with her daughter would cultivate the necessary bond Pike had been lacking her entire life. At one point, one of her mother's boyfriends whipped Pike with a belt which prompted her to wield a butcher knife against him before he was subsequently arrested. Hansen also admitted that Pike had repeatedly lied to and stolen from her. In several interviews with Hansen throughout Pike's trial and seemingly endless appeals, she admitted repeatedly that she was a terrible mother and should have spent more time with her daughter.

Pike's aunt, Carrie Ross, provided insight into Pike's upbringing when she testified that she disallowed her own children from associating with Pike because she lived in a filthy house that had zero ground rules and that Pike was a pathological liar of whom she was somewhat afraid. She also admitted that there was a history of substance abuse in Pike's family. Ross also stated that on the few occasions that Pike actually visited her she behaved like a little girl and engaged in Barbie and dress-up play with her eleven-year-old cousin. Further, there were some allegations that Pike may have been sexually abused but these were neither confirmed nor denied.

Pike's father, Glenn Pike testified that he did, in fact, kick his daughter out of his house multiple times; the last time being in 1989 after the aforementioned allegations that Pike sexually abused her two-year old half-sister. He admitted that he had signed adoption papers for Pike prior to her 18th birthday and that during the times she resided with him she was manipulative, disobedient, and dishonest.

After dropping out of high school, Pike began Job Corps classes in computer programming. Job Corps is a government-based organization that provides occupational and vocational training to underprivileged and troubled teens. It was at the now-defunct Job Corps center in Knoxville where she met Shipp, Slemmer, and Peterson. While Job Corps seeks to promote prosocial behavior and foster a strong desire among its participants to learn a vocation and secure a more promising future than might have been previously the case, this program is also known to cultivate criminal activity, likely due to the association among its participants; many of whom already had problematic behavior.

Evidence of Premeditation

On 11 January 1995, the day before the actual homicide, Pike told friend and co-Job Corps student Kim Iloilo that she was planning to kill Slemmer because she "just felt mean that day." Iloilo discounted Pike's statement as nothing more than merely talk; however, the following evening at approximately 8:00 p.m. Iloilo witnessed Pike, Shipp, Peterson, and Slemmer leaving the Job Corps center. When Iloilo saw Pike, Shipp, and Peterson returning at approximately 10:15 p.m. without Slemmer she, again, thought nothing of it. Even when Pike visited Iloilo's dorm room at 11:00 p.m. that night and confessed to killing Slemmer—as well as showing Iloilo what Pike identified as a piece of Slemmer's skull—Iloilo still failed to tell anyone. Later, at Pike's trial, Iloilo testified that while Pike was iterating the events of the murder she was oddly smiling, singing, and dancing around the room. The following morning Iloilo asked Pike what she was going to do with the piece of skull. Pike nonchalantly replied that she had it in her pocket and was, in fact, eating breakfast with it.

Pike also told another student, Stephanie Wilson, a similar account the following day and proudly described the brown spots on her shoes as blood. Not unlike Iloilo, Wilson failed to immediately report anything.

The Crime Scene

On 13 January, officers from the University of Tennessee and Knoxville Police Departments were dispatched to greenhouses on the University's agricultural campus in Tyson Park where a University grounds department employee reported finding, at approximately 8:05 a.m., what he assumed to be a dead animal. The gruesome discovery was a corpse that turned out to be Colleen Slemmer. She was naked from the waist up; her throat was cut; her head had been bludgeoned; and she had various cuts all over her arms, throat, and torso—including a pentagram that had been carved into her chest. Officer John Terry Johnson who testified at Pike's trial described Slemmer's body as so badly beaten that she was unrecognizable as a human being. He also stated that he thought he was looking at her face when, in reality, Slemmer was lying face-down in the dirt and debris where Pike, Shipp, and Peterson had left her.

There was additional evidence and testimony that the crime scene encompassed an area that measured 100 feet long by 60 feet wide; an astounding 6,000 square feet in area. Despite the area being muddy and wet there was ample evidence of a physical struggle with trampled bushes, a considerable amount of blood, body drag marks, and hand and knee prints. Thirty feet from Slemmer's body was a large pool of blood which suggested that Slemmer was attacked in one area and then dragged to where her body was later found. Slemmer's shirt and bra were also discovered at the crime scene, as well as a bloody rag that Pike admitted to tying over Slemmer's mouth at one point to keep her from screaming.

Disturbingly, University of Tennessee police officer Harold James Underwood, Jr., who was the officer assigned to secure the crime scene, testified at trial that Pike and a few other females came to the scene between four and five p.m. the day of the discovery and before Pike was even considered to be a suspect. Underwood stated that Pike had asked why the wooded area was marked off, who the victim was, and whether police had any leads as to who the suspect or suspects were. He particularly recalled Pike's odd behavior—moving around a lot while giggling amusedly—and that she wore a necklace in the shape of a pentagram. The following day, during briefing when informed that the victim had a pentagram carved into her chest, Underwood reported Pike's behavior and necklace to his supervisors.

Autopsy and Findings

During Slemmer's autopsy, the medical examiner, Dr. Sandra Elkins, had to identify the victim's body from dental records because her head was so bludgeoned that she was unrecognizable. After cleaning up Slemmer's body which was clad only in jeans, socks, and shoes, and covered with dirt and twigs, Dr. Elkins began cataloging Slemmer's wounds. Due to the sheer number of wounds on her back, arms, abdomen, and chest, and the fact that following department policy which stated that each individual wound be assigned a letter of the alphabet, when Dr. Elkins reached double letters she, instead, individually catalogued only the most serious wounds and that there were innumerable other superficial and defensive wounds. Among the most serious cuts was a six-inch gaping wound across Slemmer's throat that was deep enough to penetrate the fat and muscles in her neck as well as the aforementioned pentagram. Additional injuries included fresh bruising which Dr. Elkins asserted was consistent with crawling.

Cause of death was ultimately attributed to blunt force trauma to the head. Dr. Elkins surmised that Slemmer's head was hit with the asphalt at least four times—two to the left side, one over the right eye, and one to the nose—which collectively resulted in multiple and extensive skull fractures. One of these blows was to the left side of Slemmer's head—which, according to Dr. Elkins, occurred with the right side of the victim's head against a firm surface. This blow only fractured her skull but also imbedded a portion of Slemmer's skull into her head and contained black particles from the piece of asphalt determined to be the murder weapon.

Even more tragic was Dr. Elkins' findings that none of Slemmer's other wounds would have rendered her unconscious and evidence of active blood flow around the wounds and blood in her sinus cavity indicated that Slemmer was alive during the severe torture she suffered before being killed.

Arrest and Confession

The police quickly connected Pike to the homicide thanks to the piece of Slemmer's skull discovered in Pike's jacket pocket. Pike had left this jacket hanging on the back of a chair in Job Corps Orientation Specialist Robert A. Pollock's office on 13 January after meeting with him about a misplaced ID card. Pike's jacket remained in Pollock's office from 4:00 p.m. on 13 January until 7:30 a.m. on 17 January. After learning over the weekend that Pike was a suspect in Slemmer's murder investigation, Pollock immediately gave the jacket to William Hudson, the Job Corps' safety and security captain who turned it over to Knoxville Police Department Officer Arthur Bohanan. At trial, Bohanan would testify that he found a small piece of bone in one of the pockets and presented it to Dr. Murray Marks, a University of Tennessee forensic anthropologist who was reconstructing Slemmer's decapitated skull and the piece in Pike's jacket pocket fit perfectly into an area where a portion of her skull was missing at the time of the victim's discovery.

When confronted with this evidence and subsequently arrested, Pike waived her *Miranda* protections and confessed to the murder and permitted officers to search her dorm room where the blood-soaked jeans she wore the previous night were found. Additionally, Pike led officers to a trash can at a nearby Texaco station on Cumberland Avenue where she had disposed of Slemmer's ID and a pair of gloves Pike had been wearing at the time of the homicide.

Pike's transcribed confession was 46 pages long.

In it, Pike admitted that there was animosity between Slemmer and her because Pike was convinced that Slemmer was a rival for the affections of her boyfriend, Shipp, and that Slemmer was trying to get Pike kicked out of the Job Corps program so she could have Shipp for herself. Pike also claimed that she had awakened one night to find Slemmer standing above her with a box cutter; however, there is no evidence of this allegation. Instead, Slemmer had repeatedly called her mother, May Martinez, to tell her she was afraid of Pike who she had awakened to find in her room and that she wanted to come home; to which Slemmer's mother said that she couldn't because she had signed a contract. Pike stated that she had only planned to fight Slemmer to stop her from running her mouth. On that fateful night of 12 January, Pike, Slemmer, Shipp, and Peterson signed the Job Corps logbook as they were leaving for an outing Slemmer believed was to smoke marijuana en route to a video store so that Pike and she could try to work out their problems.

When the group entered a tunnel at the edge of Tyson Park, Slemmer likely felt that something was not quite right and proceeded to ask Pike where they were going and whether there was, in fact, any marijuana. These questions irritated Pike who began the brutal assault shortly thereafter after they had gone deeply enough into the woods so that nobody could hear them that led to Slemmer's murder.

Pike confessed to initially slamming Slemmer's head into her knee and then throwing her to the ground where Pike continually punched, kicked, and slammed Slemmer's head into the concrete, screaming, "the bi*ch won't die" and that she wanted "to see [Slemmer's] brains flow." According to witnesses Shipp and Peterson, as Slemmer continued to plead with Pike to stop, Pike got angrier and more brutal. Slemmer offered to return to her Florida home, leave her belongings at the Job Corps center, and not tell anyone what happened; however, Pike became more enraged and yelled at Slemmer to be quiet because "it was harder to hurt someone who was talking to you."

In addition to the savage beating, Slemmer had been cut innumerable times with a box cutter and a mini meat cleaver (that Pike had allegedly borrowed from another Job Corps student) to her torso, arms, face, and back including having had her throat slit six times prior to the fatal blow that resulted from having her head crushed by a piece of asphalt. There was also a pentagram carved into Slemmer's chest; however, Pike asserted that Shipp had done that. Pike also confessed to "just watching Slemmer bleed" when the victim got up and tried to run away. Pike admitted to cutting Slemmer's back: "the big long cut."

After the murder, Pike stated that she and Shipp washed their hands and shoes in a nearby mud puddle to conceal the blood, dumped the box cutter, and Pike returned the meat cleaver to the person from which she borrowed it. This person has never been identified.

The physical evidence and co-defendant testimony suggested that the assault and murder lasted from 30 minutes to an hour and consisted of Slemmer repeatedly trying to get up and run away but was prevented from doing so by the co-defendants who also, as Pike testified, contributed to the physical assault by throwing rocks at Slemmer's head and holding her down so she couldn't run away. Later, Pike would testify that she heard voices in her head overriding Slemmer's continual screaming, telling her that she needed to prevent Slemmer from filing charges against her for attempted murder. Pike also admitted that at one point she thought she had heard a noise and went to investigate it to ensure that they were alone, as well as alleging that during the assault she heard Slemmer breathing in blood and jerking but did not let this assuage her anger as Pike continued her savagery.

Even more troublesome, a police video recorded after Pike's confession shows Pike smiling and providing extensive details about the crime at the crime scene, oftentimes mimicking her actions that evening. Many have said that her demeanor on the recording was eerily similar to that of a little girl who was excited and happy that she had experienced the best day of her life and had no problem talking about the events that transpired, the heinousness of her actions, and how she felt about it all.

The facts of the homicide are not nor have they ever been in dispute, thanks to an abundance of evidence. Pike's confession, and witness testimony at the trial.

Pre-Trial Examination

Prior to her trial, Pike was given a battery of assessment tests and examined by numerous psychiatrists including clinical psychologist Dr. Eric Engum who found her to be extremely bright as evidenced by an I.Q. of 111—in the 77th percentile of the general population—which he believed to be remarkable given her difficult childhood and lack of formal schooling beyond the ninth grade. Dr. Engum also found that Pike had excellent reasoning, problem solving, language, and analytic skills, and was also quite adept at paying attention, sustaining concentration, and sequencing information. Dr. Engum concluded that Pike was legally sane and had no brain damage which has frequently been demonstrated to cause violent behavior in some individuals.

Of particular interest was that Pike was found to be marijuana- and inhalant-dependent and also diagnosed with borderline personality disorder. Whereas there are some similarities between borderline personality disorder and antisocial personality disorder such as impulsivity, irritability, aggression, and a self-image that fluctuates between self-aggrandizement and despair, there are several differences. Individuals with borderline personality disorder differ from those with antisocial behavior in that the former—which primarily affects females—is characterized by a lack of remorse, self-destructiveness, black-and-white thinking, alcohol and/or drug use or abuse, unstable relationships characterized by fear of abandonment and extreme swings between love and hate, difficulty in achieving academic and vocational goals, and are more likely to have been sexually abused; while the latter—which affects disproportionately more males—is characterized by a lack of affect and remorse, emptiness, and an ultimate goal of self-preservation.

Pike demonstrated all of the aforementioned characteristics of borderline personality disorder which makes it easier—but not justifiably so—to comprehend how her intense jealousy of Slemmer and fear of losing Shipp made her commit her atrocious acts. In addition to her fear of abandonment, Pike also abused drugs, was likely sexually abused, had contentious relationships, and displayed zero remorse. Dr. Engum surmised that Pike did not act with premeditation or deliberation in Slemmer's murder but, instead, in a manner that was consistent with borderline personality disorder. More simply, Pike had lost control. However, on cross-examination Dr. Engum admitted that Pike's deliberate luring of Slemmer, that she carved a pentagram in the victim's chest, that she brought weapons with her, and that she bashed Slemmer's head into the concrete does, in fact, constitute deliberateness.

That Pike was overjoyed and singing in Iloilo's room describing the murder while dancing around with the portion of Slemmer's skull Pike had taken as a trophy further supported Dr. Engum's diagnosis of borderline personality disorder because she had eliminated who she perceived was in competition for her boyfriend, Shipp, and, therefore, could continue her relationship with him. When questioned about the piece of skull Pike had taken, Dr. Engum said that Pike had no identity and her actions of taking and displaying the skull was a way to get recognition, no matter how misleading and distorted said recognition might be. In fact, after her conviction and sentencing Pike wrote a letter to Shipp which was intercepted by jail personnel that stated that even though she tried to be "nice" to Slemmer by bashing in her head instead of letting her bleed to death she was still sentenced to "fry."

The Trial

There was an abundance of evidence presented at the trial. Physical evidence consisted of crime scene photographs, autopsy reports, bloody clothing, and the piece of Slemmer's skull Pike had taken as a trophy. With respect to this skull piece, Dr. Elkins presented Slemmer's decapitated skull that was reconstructed by Dr. Marks to explain the victim's injuries. The skull presented at trial was complete except for a portion that was missing on the left side of Slemmer's skull. Dr. Elkins demonstrated that the piece of skull found in Pike's jacket fit perfectly into this spot, much to the chagrin of Slemmer's mother who, in a taped interview, stated that Pike was oftentimes giggling and passing notes to her mother and defense attorney during the trial, not unlike an immature middle-schooler.

At the trial, the State introduced photographs taken of Pike and Shipp at the Knoxville Police Department in which both were wearing pentagram necklaces similar to the shape carved into Slemmer's chest. It was presented that both Pike and Shipp dabbled in devil worshiping and other forms of the occult and that Slemmer was a sacrifice for the next day, Friday the 13th. Despite the presence of some type of satanic elements in Slemmer's murder, Dr. William Bernet, Vanderbilt University's psychiatric hospital medical director, testified that the evidence was that of "an adolescent dabbling in Satanism." He further concluded that the concept of collective aggression—or mob mentality—in which a group of people become stimulated and subsequently engage in some type of violent behavior was most assuredly at play in the events leading to Slemmer's death. However, Dr. Bernet ultimately stated that he did not have enough evidence to definitively surmise whether Pike had acted with premeditation or intent when she lured and murdered Slemmer.

Pike was ultimately convicted of first-degree murder and conspiracy to commit first-degree murder after a mere two-and-a-half hours of jury deliberation. The fact that the jury returned guilty verdicts for first-degree murder—and did it so quickly—demonstrate that jurors were convinced that Pike had the requisite mens rea, or mental capacity, to warrant a first-degree murder charge:

premeditation and deliberation. Amidst the overwhelming evidence and utter lack of remorse for her actions Pike was sentenced to death by electrocution (Tennessee has since adopted lethal injection for executions but has the prerogative to utilize electrocution if the lethal injection drugs cannot be obtained). Shipp was sentenced to life without parole because his age at the time of the murder was too young to warrant capital punishment and Peterson turned informant and was given six years' probation for her testimony.

Pike's conviction was upheld by the Court of Criminal Appeals and the United States Supreme Court denied certiorari.

Post-Conviction

While incarcerated, Pike demonstrated more evidence of her depravity. In 2001 she tried to murder fellow inmate Patricia Jones by strangling her with a shoelace. Pike alleges that Jones repeatedly tortured her by calling her "fried chicken" and making various demeaning sounds as an affront to what Jones said was the sound that Pike would make when she was electrocuted. The final straw was when Jones physically threatened Pike's friend, fellow devil worshiper Natasha Cornet. Pike said that she jumped atop Jones and choked her with a shoelace so that the much larger and heavier Jones would get off of Cornet. By the time prison guards reached them, Jones was unconscious.

Pike was subsequently convicted of attempted murder despite her prior death sentence because any offense committed while an individual is incarcerated must be adjudicated. During this time, neurology specialist Dr. Jonathan Henry Pincus began investigating Pike's brain to glean some type of knowledge as to why Pike behaved and continued to act violently the way she did when she assaulted Jones. He asserted that every killer he has ever examined share three commonalities: brain damage, a history of abuse, and mental illness. Dr. Pincus alleged that Pike did, in fact, possess all three features and demonstrates all of the requisite features common to serial killers.

There is much consensus among professionals that Pike would likely have been a serial killer had she not been caught the first time.

He also testified at Pike's attempted murder trial that her brain's frontal lobes are not "put together properly"; largely due, he claimed, to the fact that Pike's mother drank while she was pregnant with Pike despite denial of this by Pike's mother. It was also brought up that as a child Pike played at the slaughterhouse where her grandfather worked and that she was frequently subjected to pornography and horror movies on the home television screen. He asserted that all of these factors provide insight into how an 18-year old girl could act with such depravity as was the case when Pike murdered Slemmer. However, the original trial judge, Mary Beth Leibowitz, stated that Pincus' "findings" of brain damage was curious as the defense expert at Pike's original trial who was trying to spare her the death penalty failed to find such evidence.

Forensic psychiatrist William Kenner testified that Pike had suffered from undiagnosed bipolar disorder, the symptoms of which were evident from the time Pike was a "sleepless, talkative adolescent" and likened her to an automobile with cruise control set at 120 miles per hour. Pike's post-conviction defense team alleged that this non-diagnosis justified her requesting a new trial.

In 2002 Pike sought to have her appeal legally stopped and to proceed with her execution. In June of that year Judge Leibowitz granted Pike's request and scheduled an execution date of 19 August 2002. However, a few days later Pike changed her mind and the Tennessee Court of Appeals subsequently stayed her execution. In October 2005, Pike's death sentence was affirmed; however, no execution date has been set at this time.

Pike was again in court in 2007 when her defense team headed by Donald E. Dawson asserted sought a new trial, alleging ineffective assistance of counsel in that her trial defense team failed to introduce evidence supporting Pike's alleged bipolar disorder. During this hearing, Shipp admitted to misinforming investigators and that he, in fact, was primarily responsible for Slemmer's murder. He stated that he was drunk and tired and just wanted the police to leave him alone when he put the onus of blame on Pike. Additional testimony from prior Job Corps student and the defendants' mutual friend Tyrone Comfort stated that Shipp controlled and abused Pike despite her assertions that he was the first male to protect her and she admired the respect and fear he elicited from others. Pike, however, was heavily medicated during this hearing for her alleged bipolar condition and the hearing was rescheduled for April 2008.

During her 2008 hearing, prosecutors portrayed Pike as a cold-blooded vicious killer who not only planned Slemmer's murder but prolonged it for sport, essentially playing cat-and-mouse with Slemmer by allowing her to get up and try to escape and then pushing her back on the ground for additional torture. Ultimately, her request for a new trial was denied.

Pike became newsworthy again in 2012 when she formulated an escape plan with the help of 34-year-old New Jersey resident Donald Kohut who frequently visited Pike in prison but the extent of their relationship remains unknown, and 23-year-old former prison guard Justin Heflin. In a joint investigation by the Tennessee Department of Corrections, the Tennessee Bureau of Investigation, and the New Jersey State Police after receiving information about the plan, both men were arrested and charged with bribery and conspiracy to commit escape, with Heflin charged with an additional facilitation to commit escape charge due to his job as a prison guard. Authorities discovered contraband evidence in the facility which could have only been brought in by a staff member and that Heflin was likely involved. Further investigation demonstrated that Heflin knew Kohut and that Heflin was receiving gifts and money for his assistance in the escape plan. Pike was also charged.

Even more recently, during yet another post-conviction relief hearing in 2015, testimony revealed that Pike was allegedly pregnant at the time of the murder. While this may be true it neither excuses her actions nor provides any potential evidence of legal insanity to justify an affirmative defense of not guilty by reason of mental disease or defect or guilty but mentally ill. Also during this hearing, Slemmer's mother requested the missing piece of her daughter's skull so she could bury the whole of her daughter but was denied as the skull piece remains a critical piece of evidence in Pike's ongoing legal appeals.

Since exhausting the state appeal process, Pike's new defense attorney, Assistant Federal Defender Stephen A. Ferrell, filed a 123-page petition on her behalf alleging that he constitutional rights were violated in both the original 1996 trial and penalty phase and that Tennessee's appellate courts ignored said violations. Among these claims is that capital punishment would amount to cruel and unusual punishment in violation of the Eighth Amendment of the United States Constitution because of Pike's youth, immaturity and mental illness. While Shipp—only 17 at the time of the murder—was too young to warrant imposition of a death sentence, Pike was not. Ferrell alleged that her trial lawyers were incompetent and failed to introduce evidence of mental illness, brain injury, and post-traumatic stress disorder. In response, the state Attorney General submitted a 90-page rebuttal repeatedly asserting that the state courts' ruling were all legally correct. As of the beginning of 2016, this battle continues.

Numerous video interviews of Pike over the past several years show her admitting that she was fully cognizant of her actions and that they were wrong. She stated that she felt as though she was taking out years of abuse on Slemmer and that she committed a horrible atrocity and deserves to be punished; however, she asserts that she deserves life without the possibility of parole for her actions; not the death penalty for the actions of three individuals. She has repeatedly stated that she wishes it was she who died and not Slemmer but such protestations are moot after the fact. One cannot help but wonder if Pike actually means what she says or is simply saying what she thinks others want to her. Knoxville Police Department detective Randy York who worked the case has said that in his lengthy career he has not encountered many people who he believes are evil but that Pike is, indeed, the personification of evil and that she should never be permitted to be around other human beings ever again.

Experts assert that the death penalty is not an effective general deterrent and debate over the morality and legality of capital punishment remains contentious and in the forefront of public discourse and debate. Currently, Tennessee is only one of 38 states which have the death penalty. Whereas women comprise 13% of those arrested for murder, only 2% are sentenced to death and, of those, only 3% are actually executed; primarily due to judges not wanting to sentence women to death. In Tennessee, only two individuals on death row have been executed—both males. The last time a woman was executed in the state was in 1837. Many currently believe that Pike will likely never be executed.

THEY KILLED MOM

94

CHRISTINE GOODMAN

Nicole Kasinskas was a quiet, unassuming teenage girl. She was born and raised in Nashua, New Hampshire to Anthony Kasinskas and Jeanne Domenico.

"I lived with both of my parents and my younger brother until I was eleven years old," Nicole said. "And my parents divorced and my Dad moved out."

"I think after my parents got divorced and I was dealing with that, I became a little bit angrier. I had a little bit more resentment towards him, and it did change my perspectives about myself and about life in general, I guess even as an eleven year old."

In May of 2002, she found "romance" as a fifteen year old on-line with eighteen-year old Billy Sullivan.

Sullivan lived in a town called Willmantic where he worked as a line cook at McDonald's.

"Nicole hadn't had a lot of boyfriends," prosecuting attorney Kirsten Wilson said . "She was really caught up by the attention by this guy who was saying amazing things to her about how beautiful she was and what she meant to him."

They would communicate daily through e-mail, letters and phone calls. Despite not having met in person, they both declared love for each other within days, speaking of marriage and planning their future together.

"They filled in sort of the gaps of everyday communication and relationships with fantasies and making these assumptions on who the other person was," Wilson said.

"He lived in Connecticut and so our relationship was almost one hundred percent over the phone," Nicole said. "But it became everything to me very quickly because of the amount of attention that he paid me, and I didn't really feel that I was getting that from anywhere else."

Nicole had been vulnerable to Sullivan's Internet advances as she was a loner with very few friends in high school. She was routinely bullied at school by other girls. On one occasion, she was walking down the hall and one of her bullies had pulled her sweatpants down to her ankles. Nicole was not wearing any underwear, furthering the humiliation. Nicole refused to go back to school the next day after that incident.

"The bullying at school certainly made Nicole vulnerable to someone like Sullivan," forensic psychologist Fiona Russo said. "She's lonely, she's being picked on at school and completely humiliated. She stuck to herself and so when some guy pays attention to her, even when it is only online, her fantasy life goes into overdrive. She's able to project things on him that he doesn't deserve or merit."

The more severe the bullying became, the more Nicole began to withdraw and cling to Sullivan.

"As I got older, it was easier for me to isolate from people," Nicole said. "I think at that point I had just gotten used to being more alone as opposed to being around people. And it just became a part of who I was. Maybe if I was more open or maybe if someone had tried harder to reach out, that it could've been different."

Nicole's mom, Jeanne, was her best friend. Jeanne worked at an elementary school for a period of time, holding down such jobs as a crossing guard, a lunchroom monitor, and a paraprofessional for about three years before taking a job where she worked on group contracts for the Benefits, Brokers and Administration department.

"Jeanne Domenico was well loved in the community," Wilson said. "Hard worker. Really sort of a bright, energetic, sweet woman. She was trying to make her daughter happy."

Despite the bullying at school, Nicole got straight A's at school and made her mother happy whenever she made the honor roll.

"School really became my self-worth and I really identified with, like whatever my grades were," Nicole said. "However I was doing in school I felt it reflected on me personally, because I felt that it was so much a part of who I was. I never got in trouble in middle school. I never got spoken to. I never had a detention. It never really crossed my mind to do anything that would be against the rules."

"It would have been helpful if there was more of an acknowledgment that I was doing so well. I think it also would've been helpful if there was more involvement with guidance or something. Just more of a like a check-in...see how things are going."

"Somehow, someway, Nicole got lost in the cracks," Russo said. "That in no way justifies what she did. It may be how she justified it during this time. Her parents are divorced. She doesn't see her Dad. Her mom is working all the time. There had to have been days where she felt intense loneliness Going to school just to be ignored or bullied. To a fourteen year old girl you really may not see the light at the end of the tunnel. So you seek an outlet. Some turn to drugs. Nicole found her own drug in the form of the words that came out of Sullivan's keyboard."

MOTHER AND DAUGHTER TROUBLES

At least on the surface, there were no problems between mother and daughter.

Until Nicole ventured on-line and met Billy Sullivan.

Her mother found out about the relationship and wanting to make her daughter happy, drove the young teenager out to Connecticut so she could meet Sullivan for the first time.

"This was a two hour drive from Nashua to the place in Connecticut where Sullivan lived," Russo said. "It is easy to say here is where Jeanne made a fatal mistake. But in her mind, it is all innocent. Her daughter is fourteen and begging her to drive out to meet this guy. Begging and begging. Until she finally she relents."

More visits followed but friends and classmates knew little of the teen's relationship. Sullivan had informed some of his friends that he had a girlfriend that was "out of state." Other than that, he revealed very little about his personal life.

"He's quiet, he didn't really like to talk," recalled Danny Goss who was a classmate of Sullivan. "But he was good in school and didn't get in any trouble."

"I think the relationship intensified to a degree that Jeanne herself didn't anticipate," Russo said. "And it is easy to play Monday morning quarterback here but there had to have been some kind of father figure present to say 'hey, this is an eighteen-year old working at McDonald's. You are a fourteen year old honor student. You have a future. Don't blow it on this guy. But it isn't like teens listen to you anyway."

The two teenagers soon discussed the prospect of moving in together. Her mother quickly objected to this idea as well as nixing the idea of Nicole sharing a joint bank account with Sullivan.

But the young man later stayed overnight one weekend with Nicole's mother's full consent.

The relationship is the first for Nicole. She pedestalizes Sullivan as everything she has fantasized about is coming true.

"Nicole had a void in her life," Russo said. "When her parents divorced it certainly affected her psychologically in the way she viewed men. Then along comes Sullivan whose older and more experienced. She gets the love from him that perhaps she sought from her father. The older man, wiser than his years, showering her with attention. She was vulnerable to that."

"Her father didn't have too much to do with her after the divorce. She had that longing in her heart for that male figure. And along came Sullivan."

PERSONAL DEMONS OF HIS OWN

Sullivan, however, had his own personal demons he was fighting.

"He did have mental health issues," Wilson said. "He had been hospitalized a number of times. During high school he had some behavioral issues. Some anxiety, that kind of thing."

It was later revealed that Sullivan had been on numerous psychiatric medications to curb his depression, anger and schizophrenia. He had been weaning himself off the meds, however, and on one occasion he engaged in an argument with Nicole's mother over dinner.

Jeanne had asked Billy if she liked the dinner she had prepared. He said yes and then Jean made the comment that "I bet you don't get that too much at home."

Sullivan was highly defensive over anything that involved his home life. When Jeanne made that comment, he turned hostile.

"Sullivan was protective of his home life," Russo said. "If anyone insulted his mother or if he even perceives that someone is insulting his mother then he gets abusive. He did this to Jeanne, who had obviously made nothing more than an idle comment. That was the first warning sign and the relationship should have ended then and there."

Nicole, however, defended her young beau and from that moment the tug of war for her heart began.

"Nicole's own naivete comes to bore at this point," Russo said. "She has no experience with boys and here is this older guy that she looks up to, almost as a father figure of sorts, who turns her against her own family. Against the one person who loved her the most. Her mother. It is a tug of war that the mother loses simply because her daughter's hormones are raging and she doesn't yet have the emotional capacity to know any better."

After a year of dating, in August of 2003, Sullivan drove out to Nashua to spend a week with Nicole. By this time, they are both fed up with Nicole's mother's objections to their ideas of cohabitation.

"Our relationship was definitely emotionally abusive," Nicole said. "And I think now over time, from looking at it, my perspectives on that have changed so much. I feel like he is responsible for his actions and I am responsible for mine. I didn't really get that and I feel like in order to be emotionally abused, in order to stand for it and stay in it, there's gotta be something missing in you. There's gotta be something hurting already, something is not there, something's not right. And that needs to be figured out, found and fixed. Regardless of how a child is acting or what's coming off,there's more inside that kids need help with or guidance or just to have some type of connection with someone. You need to have relationships with people ahead of time, so that when the bad stuff does happen does happen you don't just come in to it expecting to work it out. Like, you need to have firm foundation with that person in order to work it out."

Nicole continued to side with Sullivan against her mother. The two argued constantly, Sullivan's influence quickly become apparent in Nicole's attitude toward her mother as she found fault with everything she did.

The two teens began discussing an unheard of option.

They began discussing the prospect of killing her mother.

"Well, this is where it starts getting...it's a scary business for me," Nicole said in a jailhouse interview. "I'll tell you that. I feel like I"m gonna cry. I don't talk about this stuff so this is really the first time. I think that my relationship with my mom was good. It was fine. I loved my mom. And...that changed. When...I'm not saying I stopped loving my mom, but...our relationship changed. I'm not gonna say that we were the most open because we weren't. We didn't talk about every little thing. I don't remember ever once talking about my parents' divorce with either of them. But the thing is, we didn't really talk about much of anything. When I was fourteen, I became involved with seventeen year old boy. This is really stemming into why I'm here (in jail) now."

OUT OF CONTROL

"Emotions begin to run high as Sullivan ups the ante in his hatred for Nicole's mother," Russo said. "Nicole is emotionally underdeveloped and has to choose between her mother and her 'man.' It is easy to look at it hindsight but with the teenaged girl's warp logic, she sees Sullivan as her entire world now. So she will do anything for him. Even murder."

Nicole's mom really didn't realize the danger that Sullivan was. She began doing what every mom does, demanding that her daughter stop seeing him, stop chatting with him and concentrate on her schoolwork. Nicole, on the other hand, remained fervent in her desire to move to Connecticut to move in with Sullivan.

"Jeanie, rightfully so, said 'you're fifteen you're finishing school,'" Wilson said. "'You're not moving to Connecticut' and that really upset both Nicole and Billy."

The prospect of not seeing Nicole had an adverse emotional effect on Billy.

"He started talking about killing himself...on the road...driving into a big truck because of leaving me..because of his sadness over it," Nicole recalled. "And I think now it just sounds silly, you know? But it wasn't then, and it was terrifying to me because I didn't...I didn't know how to...because of the way that our relationship was. Because he had become so much a part of my life. I mean, I really didn't feel like I was anything without him. I had nothing in my life at that time...I felt...at that time. So the thought of losing him in that way just wasn't okay with me. And that is unfortunately when conversations started about ultimately what happened. I guess I really I don't really go into too many details but I was sixteen and he was eighteen at that time. And I guess I should give you some background. He killed my mom and I was a part of it. I was not physically there but I knew and I helped him. I was, you know, going through the motions of what was being done. But mentally and emotionally, I don't think I was fully there. I don't think I was fully getting it."

"It was emotional manipulation," Russo said. "It is all so scary romantic for a fifteen year old girl to have some guy who is so in love with her that he is going to kill himself because he can't be with her. She has no one in her life to say 'this guy is a loser nutcase.' There isn't anyone that can talk sense to her. So she falls for the emotional manipulation of a highly disturbed but cunning con man."

Billy had convinced the depressed Nicole that her mother was an obstacle to both hers and his happiness.

"I really just did whatever I could to maintain that relationship because I didn't want to lose that," Nicole said. "I didn't want to lose him. And I quickly learned how it would go if I didn't always do everything that he wanted me to do. At that point...you know, getting to be fifteen...sixteen years old...I would fight more with my mom and there was a lot more to fight about, especially with, you know, this relationship that I was having with this kid."

THE FINAL PLAN

The couple tried different methods to murder Jeanne Domenico.

First they tried to poison Jeanne's coffee. The teens had placed Dimetapp, Benadryl and other drugs into Jeanne's coffee creamer in the refrigerator.

Jeanne used the creamer but didn't die and evidently remained ignorant of the plot on her life. The teens then added bleach to the creamer, wanting to strengthen the amount of poison. It was unclear in a court affidavit if Jeanne ever drank from the spiked creamer again.

The next idea was to set Nicole's mattress on fire with a candle. That idea didn't work because the bedding was made of fire retardant material.

It is unclear how the teens planned to fire up the mattress, whether they sneaked into her Nicole's bedroom and tried to fire up the mattress while she slept.

The third idea was to blow up the fuel oil tank in Jeanne's house. The teens had tied two ropes together which would serve as a wick. Their idea was to set fire to the rope which would then ignite a fire from the fuel tank. This idea was of course unsuccessful.

"These were hair-brained schemes from the start," Russo said, "particularly the fuel tank episode. What is interesting is that these are passive attacks. There is no face to face encounter with the mother, they just really want her gone. But it does show how these were test-runs of sorts. Sullivan was working up his nerve to do something violent. Nicole was building up her psyche. With each unsuccessful dry run, their determination and focus to do the job became greater until finally they realized that physical violence would be the only alternative."

THE ATTACK

The couple decided that Sullivan would do the killing. Nicole waited in the car at a local 7-Eleven where he mother worked part time to make ends meet. She wanted to wait there because she hated her home so much. Her boyfriend obliged, and entered the home of Jeanne Domenico between the hours of six and seven in the evening, waiting for her to come home from work.

The plan was for Billy to kill Jeanne by hitting her on the back of her head with a baseball bat.

Nicole waited anxiously in the car for an extended period of time then began to get worried as to why Sullivan was taking so long.

"Nicole called him and asked him what was taking so long," Wilson said. "Jeanne began getting upset that Nicole wasn't home and kept saying 'where is she? Tell her to come home.'"

Nicole heard her mother's voice on the other end of her cell phone telling her to "come home."

As became her habit, she did not listen to her mother.

"Sullivan did not attack Jeanne immediately," Russo said. "Again, he needed that fuel to add to his fire. So he confronted Jeanne, asking her why they kept refusing them to be together. Jeanne would speak logically like any adult would. She's underage. She's still in school. Of course, none of this would get into the head of Sullivan."

Jeanne made the mistake of turning her back on the young man. He then hit her across the back with the baseball bat.

"It looks as if Jeanne tried to get out of the kitchen door," Wilson said. "Billy started grabbing kitchen knives and attacking Jeanne with the steak knives from the state clock in the kitchen."

The attack was, in a word, brutal.

Sullivan stabbed Jeanne numerous times near her heart and stomach. He stabbed with such ferocity that the blade broke off the knife and he had to retrieve another. Then he stabbed her eight times in the throat.

"A number of the steak knives snapped off during the course of the attack," Wilson said.

According to later testimony by Sullivan, Jeanne managed to get a hold of one of the knives and tried to fight back. At this point, however, she is stunned and bleeding. Sullivan realizes that he is in trouble and goes in to finish the job.

Sullivan stabs her repeatedly as Jeanne tries to get away. A blade enters her lung.

"I'm done," were Jeanne's final words.

He then changed his clothes and cleaned the blood off. He then went back to Nicole, telling her to go inside the house to check for any weapons that he may have left behind. He also told her to get a towel.

The murder complete, Sullivan returned to the vehicle and announced that he had done the deal.

The couple, however, had a deal. It was now time for Nicole to do her part. She would help clean up the evidence left behind.

"The fact that she could go and clean up after Billy had killed her mother," Wilson said. "She had to have hit her mother with the door. And then she had to have stepped over her body to clean up for her boyfriend. That she was able to do that was chilling to do me."

Nicole took a cloth and began clean up her mother's blood from the kitchen floor.

"The fact that a psychopath like Sullivan was able to stab Jeanne to death isn't the most blood curdling aspect of this case," Russo said. "The really scary part is how Nicole was able to go back into that house, see her mother laying in a pool of blood on the kitchen floor, then begin to do her end of the bargain, which was to clean up after her boyfriend. The amount of psychological and emotional disconnect here is chilling."

The two then hid the evidence in the outskirts around town before going to a shopping mall in order for Sullivan to purchase new clothes.

Hours after the killing, Nicole finally began to realize the gravity of what has taken place. She realizes that she and Billy were not going off to "see the world." Her best friend, her mother was gone forever.

Jeanne's body would be discovered by her boyfriend later that evening and he quickly called the police. At around 10:15 p.m., Sergeant William Moore and Detective Shawn Hill saw Sullivan and Nicole approach the crime scene.

"They were cocky enough to think they could outwit the cops," Russo said. "By approaching the crime scene and acting all innocent, not knowing what happened, they thought they would deflect attention away from themselves. It really shows you how dumb these two kids were."

The police then stated the teens would have to be separated for an interview. Nicole protested, stating that Sullivan would not know how to get to the police station. The police informed her that they would take him there themselves.

"This is when things start to go haywire in their heads," Russo said. "Nicole is getting nervous, knowing that they will be questioned separately and face the prospect of not having their stories straight. These two were not exactly forward thinking individuals."

The two waited for the police cruisers to arrive and made conversation with Detective Moore. The detective noted that Sullivan did most all of the talking and admitted that he did not like police officers, stating that he had been charged before with crimes he did not commit.

Moore informed Sullivan that he would be given a "fair shake" in the questioning.

Sullivan, however, kept talking. He informed the detective that he had been shopping for souvenirs with Nicole that day and talked about Jeanne's relationship with Nicole. The detective said that Sullivan paced back and forth and then sat down on the trunk of his car.

Twelve minutes later, Detective Linehan arrived on the scene, making contact with both Nicole and Sullivan. Linehan noticed how nervous and "jumpy" Sullivan was. Linehan told Sullivan to "relax" and then the teen explained that he suffered from anxiety but did not need medication. He told the police that he had "no problem" to come to the station for questioning.

Linehan sat with Sullivan in the back seat of the squad car as they headed back to the station. Both of the teens were having casual conversations with the officers but after being questioned separately, they both admitted their involvement, leading police to the locations where they had disposed of the evidence.

"Both of the teenage lovers wilted under the police interrogations," Russo said. "She immediately ratted out Sullivan as the killer while he did the same to her. There was no loyalty for one another while under the police questioning."

Sullivan would be convicted of first degree murder, sentenced to life without parole.

Sullivan, however, did not let his Lothario ways go to rust in jail. He wrote love letters to a girl named Monique Teal who was then sixteen. This occurred while Sullivan was awaiting trial and later Teal's testimony was used in court.

Teal, using a pen name of Monique Sullivan in her love letters to Sullivan, had agreed to a date to marry the now twenty-year old murderer. Teal's mother, however, found out about the letters and forbade him to call or write.

"He just laughed about it," she said. "He said that no matter what my mom would say or do that nothing could keep us away from each other."

"You see him trying the same techniques on Teal," Russo said. "The immediate declarations of love. The flowery language. The idea of them against the world. In Teal's case, however, her mother put a stop to it."

Sullivan admitted to the Jeanne Domenico killing in one of his letters to her, Teal would reveal, although she didn't read from the letter in court. She said she obeyed Sullivan's demands and threw that letter away.

JAIL LIFE

Nicole Kasinskas would plead guilty to second-degree murder.

"My original sentence was forty years to life," Nicole said. "It is now thirty-seven years and a half to life based on a plea that if I acquired my GED I would get two and a half years off. I don't mark days off on my calendar. I don't do those types of things. This is my life now and I want to live it. I don't want to just look at it as one day down closer to my real life. Like this is my real life. I smile a lot and I live a lot and I'm happy a lot and I just prefer it that way rather than get lost in the sadness of it because you can. And I have. But if I...if I can choose not to...if I can be stronger than than then I want to. And it makes me feel freer. It makes me feel that I have more control of my life."

"Her life as a promising honor roll student at fifteen years old with her mother who loved her very much," Wilson said. "She lost her entire life. And for what?"

"I had no goals. I had no hopes and dreams, you know? You need to have your own hobbies and friends and stuff. Outside the relationship, there needs to be that balance. I just never had that, I never figured that out."

"Maybe if someone had said something like, 'I see you, I see that there's more to you than this and I want to see more of you. I'm here for you. I care about you.' I mean everyone needs help, everyone needs support."

A MOTHER'S KILLER : THE TRUE STORY OF JENNIFER BAILEY

AMBER ULLMER

Imagine coming home after a hard day of work through the door to your quarter of a million dollar home. Then, hearing an eerie silence and nothing but darkness surrounding every inch of your four bedroom, two bathroom, roomy home. With a passing glance to the dining room and living room of your 3400-square-foot house, you head up the stairs with the goal of taking a warm bath and getting a fresh set of clothes for the night.

This is what Susan Bailey[1] did just before it happened. Two dozen stab wounds and two slashes to her throat cut that goal short with a spattering of blood on the wall and a coagulating pool of blood beneath her. She didn't expect to be killed that night. Neither did she expect it to be her own children who would do it to her.

Susan Marie Bailey grew up as a bubbly, funny, outgoing, and smart kid, according to her mother, Kate Morten. She had curly dark hair, was the second of four kids, and was extremely musically talented with the violin and clarinet. Susan was always a people-person. She wanted to do something at the intersection of business, fashion, and people. So, she went to college and earned a business and accounting degree at her local Minnesota college.

---

1.   http://www.apple.com/

To get her fashion experience, Susan worked at Levi Strauss & Co. while in college. She still wanted to get out there more. Her life was a struggle in Minnesota with the snow stomping on her every attempt to be successful. She couldn't make it to work during the winter and work didn't stop just for the weather.

Susan had a difficult time commuting to work. She had to struggle through twenty miles of snow and ice every day. Months and months of brutal winter weather created snow drifts and blinding blizzards that became a routine. She requested to be moved to a closer store which they allowed her to do. Even though it became easier because she didn't have to drive that far in that bad of weather through the winter, it wasn't any easier in the Spring. An extra 28 inches of snow replaced pleasant Spring weather.

Then, one time when she had to close up shop after the other customers left and the cleaning had been done, she locked the front door and discovered an empty parking lot. Well, almost empty. Snow took over everything in sight, including her car.

Snow chilled her to the bone, darkness swallowed the town, and she was all alone. The snow was so high that she couldn't even open the doors to her car to get inside. So, she called her parents from a pay phone in a state of panic. She cried and in a fit of shivering from the cold she told her mother, "I'm never going to spend another winter in Minnesota." She did just that.

With that, Susan moved to California and built a successful clothing store. Then, she met her husband, Richard Bailey. Not so long after, she called up her mom with a startling message. "Mom, I'm married," Susan told her mother over a phone call in 1988, "Richard and I eloped."

Richard worked in the military and Susan was forced to follow him around while he was in the military. After he finished with the military, he took over caring for his kids and Susan worked. She worked extremely hard and took good care of her kids: Jennifer and David.

She worked two jobs to make sure that her kids could have anything and everything they ever wanted. Problems started when Jennifer was 18 and she wanted a 16-year-old guy named Paul Henson Jr. He was into Satanism, songs about death, and role-playing games. Of course, Jennifer's mother wasn't so thrilled about this and forbid her daughter to see the boy.

Similarly, 14-year-old Merrilee White wanted to be with Jennifer's boyfriend and she was willing to go to great lengths to do so. Her mother, Amy White, also didn't like Paul and told her not to see him. Meanwhile, little David Bailey just wanted to make his sister happy who oftentimes had to take care of him because the mom worked so much.

According to Donna Fielder, author of "Ladykiller," Paul Henson convinced the two that he had two personalities. Apparently, each girl was dating one of them.

Jennifer was scheduled to begin at an art college in a few days and the other three were supposed to start at Northwest Independent School District. Under the veil of appearing to be innocent teenagers, the four of them plotted for days. They planned on killing their parents so they could all be together, drive to Canada, and live happily ever after.

Paul, a 16-year-old with a double personality in which one was an executioner from the 18th century, had been dying to kill someone anyway. He wanted to know what it was like. So, Merrilee attempted to stab her sleeping mother who luckily talked her out of trying to stab her, Paul waited at home with a gun for his parents, and Jennifer Bailey waited at home for her hard-working mom to get home so she could kill her.

Jennifer Bailey was the only successful one out of the three. Susan Bailey was just coming home after leaving her second job in Fort Worth, Texas for the day. She returned home just in time. Jen, Paul, and David took turns stabbing Susan 26 times in the throat after Paul's attempt to kill his parents didn't work.

On September 29, 2008, 11:31 AM, it was reported that 43-year-old Susan Bailey was found dead in her Roanoke home. The Tarrant County Medical Examiner's office claimed that she had multiple stab wounds to her neck. According to star-telegram.com, "Sgt. Chris Almonrode said officers had visited her home in the 200 block of Oxford Drive on Friday at the request of the woman's mother, who had grown concerned after not hearing from her daughter. He said officers could not get an answer at the door and found no evidence indicating that anything was wrong."

Kate Morten, Susan's mother, tried calling her daughter from her home in Minnesota. When no one answered, she called the Roanoke, Texas police. No one came to the door of their upscale home, so the Roanoke police burst into the door and found a murder scene.

They found the mother's body upstairs in the hallway sitting in a pool of her own blood. Foul play was immediately suspected as the cause of death. The Texas officers also found a bowl of poisoned pudding, a chunk of hair, and an electrical cord dangling right into a bathtub. Inside the bathtub sat three phones and a knife under a foot of water. Jennifer and David were going to kill their mother one way or another.

Meanwhile, a curious South Dakota cop stopped Susan's car for violating town curfew and couldn't believe what he found. He pulled over Jennifer Bailey, 14-year-old David, and 16-year-old Paul in Susan's 2002 Saturn. He pulled them over at a closed gas station where they were trying to steal gas. They didn't have any money and their stories didn't make much sense. They had no real plan either.

He took them to the station and called the police in Roanoke, Texas. They knew about the kids and the woman that the car was registered to. The Tuesday before that week, Paul's father reported him a runaway and thought he was at Jennifer's house. The officers did not find him there. They did find his packed bags and a driver's license. Later on that day, they came back when Susan found a loaded magazine for a pistol, but the police couldn't find the gun.

Roanoke officers quickly put the pieces together after hearing that the three were together in Susan's car. At first, they didn't go straight in when the mother called worried about Susan because no one came to the door and the car was gone. When they found out about the kids, that's when they went in through the house through a window and found the dead mother.

The officer called Roanoke police and upon hearing what was happening, he held the three on suspicion of capital murder. They were all held at a juvenile detention facility in Sioux Falls, S.D.

Paul wasn't able to kill his parents, they decided to stay out late for a dinner and a movie, thankfully. Merrilee White, on the other hand, didn't get to kill her mother Amy White because luckily, she woke up before she could. The 15-year-old Fort Worth girl was detained on the 23rd of September after her mother reported that she woke up and found the girl standing over her with a knife. Merrilee was demanding that Amy give her her car keys. The girl later admitted to the police that she wanted to take her mother's car so that could take her friends to Canada.

When authorities went to investigate[2], they found notebooks, binders, and handwritten papers, computers, and discs that police described as, "pertaining to the preparation of murder." In the boyfriend's home, they found handwritten notes, papers, computers, discs, and "The Demonic Bible." As mentioned earlier, Paul loved to practice Satanism and was fond of all the things any parents wouldn't want their 17-year-old to be into. He was an avid fan of role-playing and fantasized frequently. Only, this wasn't done as a result of the fantasizing mind of a deranged 17-year-old; it was real.

---

2.   http://www.nbcdfw.com/news/local/

Affidavits_4_Teens_Planned_To_Kill_N_Texas_Mom.html

On September 23rd, police called the Bailey home because they were looking for the boyfriend who was reported as a runaway. Susan and Jennifer fought over Paul. Police later came back later when Susan reported finding ammunition. The police searched the home and found a butcher knife in between the couch cushions and a knife under Jennifer's bed. Jennifer was showing signs of plans to kill early enough that it could have been prevented. However, her sweet mother had no clue that Jen would actually kill her.

Their school district, Northwest Independent School District, commented on this in an article published on September 29th in 2008 at approximately 11:31 AM. They said, "Our thoughts are with the families involved, and our school personnel continue to focus on the education and well being of our students. Should any child or staff member need to talk about the situation, school counselors are available." Too bad their counselors didn't notice earlier how unstable these four children were. Susan Bailey might still be alive.

Donna Fielder, as mentioned later, spoke to Kate, Susan's mom, who said that she still couldn't believe that her grandchildren would do such a terrible thing. Kate lived through the moment with baited breath from the phone call that drew silence from her deceased daughter to the announcement that her grandchildren killed their mother, her daughter.

What happened to the other three kids? [3]Jen stayed in the Denton County jail without bail and the boys stayed at the Denton Country Juvenile Facility. All three faced capital murder charges. They even tried to try Paul as an adult. In this case, he would serve out his Juvenile sentence and then finish up his sentence as an adult afterward. Under normal conditions[4], juvenile offenders were released from Texas Youth Commission when they would become adults so they could serve out

---

3.   http://www.nbcdfw.com/news/local/

   Affidavits_4_Teens_Planned_To_Kill_N_Texas_Mom.html

4.   http://crimeblog.dallasnews.com/2008/12/roanoke-woman-indicted-in-moth.html/

the rest of their sentence. Davide was tried under state's determinate sentencing statute.

Paul got 60 years in prison[5], Jennifer got 60 years in prison, and David only did his juvenile term then went on to live as normal a life as he could have. When police asked Jennifer about her motive, she simply said, "We did not see eye to eye."

It seems like such a small charge for murderers. Would a life-sentence have been more deserved? Probably. Did they get a light charge because they were only kids? Most likely.

My Life of Crime [6]laid out the details in regards to the three murderers. Jennifer Bailey is a white female born on October 5th, 1990. Her maximum sentence date is September, 26th, 2068 which she has been sentenced to spend at Hilltop Unit. Hilltop Unit[7]. is a correctional institutions division (prison) located at 1500 State School Road, Gatesville, TX 76598-2996. It can be found three miles outside of Gatesville.

On The Texas Tribune[8], Jennifer Bailey is listed as being located at the Mountain View Unit for committing "LESSER INCLU MURDER committed on 9/26/2008 in Denton County" for which she is serving a "60-year term" beginning on "9/26/1008."

She is listed as a female, at 25 years of age, found in Mountain View under 01621147, from Denton county, and born 10/5/1990. She is white, 5 ft 5 in, 122 lbs, with blonde hair and hazel eyes.

Her parole eligibility date is 9/26/2038.

On *Denton County, TX Jail Records*, Paul Allen Henson Jr. is listed with the aliases of "Talos, Malaki, and Scai" with an SO# of 164000,

---

5.   http://www.apple.com/

6.   https://mylifeofcrime.wordpress.com/2012/12/07/kids-that-kill-jennifer-bailey-david-bailey-and-paul-allen-henson-jr/

7.   https://www.tdcj.state.tx.us/unit_directory/ht.html

8.   https://www.texastribune.org/library/data/texas-prisons/inmates/jennifer-bailey/727001/

and he is described as a white male with brown hair/eyes standing 6'3"
at 145 pounds. He was booked at the Denton County Sheriff's Office
on 06/09/2009 for capital murder by terror threat/other felony. His
offense date is 09/26/2008. Because he has to spend 60 years in jail, he's
looking to be released 9/26/2068.

A few years later, Candice Delong sat down in an interview with
Jennifer Bailey for the details on Jennifer's perspective that night when
they killed Susan Bailey.

During the video,[9] Jennifer says that she went upstairs and started
feeling doubtful. She went upstairs to the bathroom and looked at
herself good in the face. Jennifer knew she would have to look at that
face for the rest of her life and the decision she was about to make.

She questioned if she really wanted to kill her mother. She
explained, "That is when I made the decision that I was going to tell
my mom what was going to happen and then call the police regardless
of the consequences." She then said that she was too late. She heard a
scream that broke her thought processes. She went out to the hallway
and found her mother pushed up against the wall by Paul who had one
hand around her throat and a knife in the other.

Jennifer Bailey then says that her mother told her to "call the
police." She adds, "Then I said no."

Explaining why, she said, "Because, at the same time, Paul pointed
at me and said, 'Don't!' And to this day, I have no idea why I said, 'no.'
After I said, 'no,' Paul just grins and pulls the knife across her throat."
From there, Jennifer and David helped finish the mother off. With
that, they took off with the mother's car, no money, and whatever gas
was in the tank to get them to Canada.

Donna Fielder, the woman who originally covered this story when
working at the local newspaper in the Bailey's hometown, recalls the
event in September 2008 that ended with the death of Susan Bailey
at the hands of four teenagers. She explains how the four of them:

9.　　http://www.investigationdiscovery.com/tv-shows/facing-evil/videos/jennifer-bailey/

Jennifer Bailey, David Bailey, Paul Henson, and Merrilee White tried to kill their parents and steal whatever money they could from them before taking their cars they planned on driving all the way to Canada from Texas.

She recalls that the four teenagers plotted against Susan Bailey, a hard-working mother, and the long journey they made from her death to that run-down gas station they were pulled over at.

Jennifer Bailey, David Bailey, Merrilee White, and Paul Allen Henson enacted one of the most violent crimes in US history to a woman who did not deserve such an attack. It was such a popular case that filmmakers have taken to the story and made video-enactments of it such as *Deadly Women,* a series that took Jennifer Bailey's story and portrayed her as a young girl who fell in love with a pagan, Paul. Paul convinces Bailey to kill her mother and run off with him. They plan on running off to Canada together, but it doesn't quite go as planned. The mother tells her they cannot speak and havoc wreaks as Paul tells Jennifer that she needs to brutally murder her mother.

Susan Bailey was a hard working mother of Jennifer and David who had anything and everything they ever wanted until Paul came into the picture and what they had was just not enough.

Jennifer and Merrilee were bound so tight under the spell of Paul and David just wanted to make his sister happy. With that, they took a sharp blade and took away Susan's life and breath. They tried to get away and enjoy a happy life in the cold of Canada, but they lacked a plan and cash to make that fantasy a truth.

Perhaps this was all the will of a psychopathic teenager who thought he was two people. Sadly, he ruined the lives of two young girls and a young boy to fulfill his disgusting fantasies.

To this day, David and Merrilee sit alone and forgotten and without the ones they loved. Jennifer and Paul await 52 years more of time to stare at bars and cement walls. David lost a sister, a mother, and two friends. Merrilee lost three friends and the trust of her mother. Paul lost two loving parents and both his girlfriends. Jennifer lost the most: her boyfriend who she cared for dearly, her mother, and her self-worth.

The moral of the story? The all-American family, neighbors, children aren't all that movies and books make them be. Darkness taints the pages of every good storybook.

A MOTHER'S KILLER :

THE TRUE STORY OF NICOLE KASINSKAS

120

CHRISTINE GOODMAN

Nicole Kasinskas was a quiet, unassuming teenage girl. She was born and raised in Nashua, New Hampshire to Anthony Kasinskas and Jeanne Domenico.

"I lived with both of my parents and my younger brother until I was eleven years old," Nicole said. "And my parents divorced and my Dad moved out."

"I think after my parents got divorced and I was dealing with that, I became a little bit angrier. I had a little bit more resentment towards him, and it did change my perspectives about myself and about life in general, I guess even as an eleven year old."

In May of 2002, she found "romance" as a fifteen year old on-line with eighteen-year old Billy Sullivan.

Sullivan lived in a town called Willmantic where he worked as a line cook at McDonald's.

"Nicole hadn't had a lot of boyfriends," prosecuting attorney Kirsten Wilson said . "She was really caught up by the attention by this guy who was saying amazing things to her about how beautiful she was and what she meant to him."

They would communicate daily through e-mail, letters and phone calls. Despite not having met in person, they both declared love for each other within days, speaking of marriage and planning their future together.

"They filled in sort of the gaps of everyday communication and relationships with fantasies and making these assumptions on who the other person was," Wilson said.

"He lived in Connecticut and so our relationship was almost one hundred percent over the phone," Nicole said. "But it became everything to me very quickly because of the amount of attention that he paid me, and I didn't really feel that I was getting that from anywhere else."

Nicole had been vulnerable to Sullivan's Internet advances as she was a loner with very few friends in high school. She was routinely bullied at school by other girls. On one occasion, she was walking down the hall and one of her bullies had pulled her sweatpants down to her ankles. Nicole was not wearing any underwear, furthering the humiliation. Nicole refused to go back to school the next day after that incident.

"The bullying at school certainly made Nicole vulnerable to someone like Sullivan," forensic psychologist Fiona Russo said. "She's lonely, she's being picked on at school and completely humiliated. She stuck to herself and so when some guy pays attention to her, even when it is only online, her fantasy life goes into overdrive. She's able to project things on him that he doesn't deserve or merit."

The more severe the bullying became, the more Nicole began to withdraw and cling to Sullivan.

"As I got older, it was easier for me to isolate from people," Nicole said. "I think at that point I had just gotten used to being more alone as opposed to being around people. And it just became a part of who I was. Maybe if I was more open or maybe if someone had tried harder to reach out, that it could've been different."

Nicole's mom, Jeanne, was her best friend. Jeanne worked at an elementary school for a period of time, holding down such jobs as a crossing guard, a lunchroom monitor, and a paraprofessional for about three years before taking a job where she worked on group contracts for the Benefits, Brokers and Administration department.

"Jeanne Domenico was well loved in the community," Wilson said. "Hard worker. Really sort of a bright, energetic, sweet woman. She was trying to make her daughter happy."

Despite the bullying at school, Nicole got straight A's at school and made her mother happy whenever she made the honor roll.

"School really became my self-worth and I really identified with, like whatever my grades were," Nicole said. "However I was doing in school I felt it reflected on me personally, because I felt that it was so much a part of who I was. I never got in trouble in middle school. I never got spoken to. I never had a detention. It never really crossed my mind to do anything that would be against the rules."

"It would have been helpful if there was more of an acknowledgment that I was doing so well. I think it also would've been helpful if there was more involvement with guidance or something. Just more of a like a check-in...see how things are going."

"Somehow, someway, Nicole got lost in the cracks," Russo said. "That in no way justifies what she did. It may be how she justified it during this time. Her parents are divorced. She doesn't see her Dad. Her mom is working all the time. There had to have been days where she felt intense loneliness Going to school just to be ignored or bullied. To a fourteen year old girl you really may not see the light at the end of the tunnel. So you seek an outlet. Some turn to drugs. Nicole found her own drug in the form of the words that came out of Sullivan's keyboard."

MOTHER AND DAUGHTER TROUBLES

At least on the surface, there were no problems between mother and daughter.

Until Nicole ventured on-line and met Billy Sullivan.

Her mother found out about the relationship and wanting to make her daughter happy, drove the young teenager out to Connecticut so she could meet Sullivan for the first time.

"This was a two hour drive from Nashua to the place in Connecticut where Sullivan lived," Russo said. "It is easy to say here is where Jeanne made a fatal mistake. But in her mind, it is all innocent. Her daughter is fourteen and begging her to drive out to meet this guy. Begging and begging. Until she finally she relents."

More visits followed but friends and classmates knew little of the teen's relationship. Sullivan had informed some of his friends that he had a girlfriend that was "out of state." Other than that, he revealed very little about his personal life.

"He's quiet, he didn't really like to talk," recalled Danny Goss who was a classmate of Sullivan. "But he was good in school and didn't get in any trouble."

"I think the relationship intensified to a degree that Jeanne herself didn't anticipate," Russo said. "And it is easy to play Monday morning quarterback here but there had to have been some kind of father figure present to say 'hey, this is an eighteen-year old working at McDonald's. You are a fourteen year old honor student. You have a future. Don't blow it on this guy. But it isn't like teens listen to you anyway."

The two teenagers soon discussed the prospect of moving in together. Her mother quickly objected to this idea as well as nixing the idea of Nicole sharing a joint bank account with Sullivan.

But the young man later stayed overnight one weekend with Nicole's mother's full consent.

The relationship is the first for Nicole. She pedestalizes Sullivan as everything she has fantasized about is coming true.

"Nicole had a void in her life," Russo said. "When her parents divorced it certainly affected her psychologically in the way she viewed men. Then along comes Sullivan whose older and more experienced. She gets the love from him that perhaps she sought from her father. The older man, wiser than his years, showering her with attention. She was vulnerable to that."

"Her father didn't have too much to do with her after the divorce. She had that longing in her heart for that male figure. And along came Sullivan."

PERSONAL DEMONS OF HIS OWN

Sullivan, however, had his own personal demons he was fighting.

"He did have mental health issues," Wilson said. "He had been hospitalized a number of times. During high school he had some behavioral issues. Some anxiety, that kind of thing."

It was later revealed that Sullivan had been on numerous psychiatric medications to curb his depression, anger and schizophrenia. He had been weaning himself off the meds, however, and on one occasion he engaged in an argument with Nicole's mother over dinner.

Jeanne had asked Billy if she liked the dinner she had prepared. He said yes and then Jean made the comment that "I bet you don't get that too much at home."

Sullivan was highly defensive over anything that involved his home life. When Jeanne made that comment, he turned hostile.

"Sullivan was protective of his home life," Russo said. "If anyone insulted his mother or if he even perceives that someone is insulting his mother then he gets abusive. He did this to Jeanne, who had obviously made nothing more than an idle comment. That was the first warning sign and the relationship should have ended then and there."

Nicole, however, defended her young beau and from that moment the tug of war for her heart began.

"Nicole's own naivete comes to bore at this point," Russo said. "She has no experience with boys and here is this older guy that she looks up to, almost as a father figure of sorts, who turns her against her own family. Against the one person who loved her the most. Her mother. It is a tug of war that the mother loses simply because her daughter's hormones are raging and she doesn't yet have the emotional capacity to know any better."

After a year of dating, in August of 2003, Sullivan drove out to Nashua to spend a week with Nicole. By this time, they are both fed up with Nicole's mother's objections to their ideas of cohabitation.

"Our relationship was definitely emotionally abusive," Nicole said. "And I think now over time, from looking at it, my perspectives on that have changed so much. I feel like he is responsible for his actions and I am responsible for mine. I didn't really get that and I feel like in order to be emotionally abused, in order to stand for it and stay in it, there's gotta be something missing in you. There's gotta be something hurting already, something is not there, something's not right. And that needs to be figured out, found and fixed. Regardless of how a child is acting or what's coming off,there's more inside that kids need help with or guidance or just to have some type of connection with someone. You need to have relationships with people ahead of time, so that when the bad stuff does happen does happen you don't just come in to it expecting to work it out. Like, you need to have firm foundation with that person in order to work it out."

Nicole continued to side with Sullivan against her mother. The two argued constantly, Sullivan's influence quickly become apparent in Nicole's attitude toward her mother as she found fault with everything she did.

The two teens began discussing an unheard of option.

They began discussing the prospect of killing her mother.

"Well, this is where it starts getting...it's a scary business for me," Nicole said in a jailhouse interview. "I'll tell you that. I feel like I"m gonna cry. I don't talk about this stuff so this is really the first time. I think that my relationship with my mom was good. It was fine. I loved my mom. And...that changed. When...I'm not saying I stopped loving my mom, but...our relationship changed. I'm not gonna say that we were the most open because we weren't. We didn't talk about every little thing. I don't remember ever once talking about my parents' divorce with either of them. But the thing is, we didn't really talk about much of anything. When I was fourteen, I became involved with seventeen year old boy. This is really stemming into why I'm here (in jail) now."

OUT OF CONTROL

"Emotions begin to run high as Sullivan ups the ante in his hatred for Nicole's mother," Russo said. "Nicole is emotionally underdeveloped and has to choose between her mother and her 'man.' It is easy to look at it hindsight but with the teenaged girl's warp logic, she sees Sullivan as her entire world now. So she will do anything for him. Even murder."

Nicole's mom really didn't realize the danger that Sullivan was. She began doing what every mom does, demanding that her daughter stop seeing him, stop chatting with him and concentrate on her schoolwork. Nicole, on the other hand, remained fervent in her desire to move to Connecticut to move in with Sullivan.

"Jeanie, rightfully so, said 'you're fifteen you're finishing school,'" Wilson said. "'You're not moving to Connecticut' and that really upset both Nicole and Billy."

The prospect of not seeing Nicole had an adverse emotional effect on Billy.

"He started talking about killing himself...on the road...driving into a big truck because of leaving me..because of his sadness over it," Nicole recalled. "And I think now it just sounds silly, you know? But it wasn't then, and it was terrifying to me because I didn't...I didn't know how to...because of the way that our relationship was. Because he had become so much a part of my life. I mean, I really didn't feel like I was anything without him. I had nothing in my life at that time...I felt...at that time. So the thought of losing him in that way just wasn't okay with me. And that is unfortunately when conversations started about ultimately what happened. I guess I really I don't really go into too many details but I was sixteen and he was eighteen at that time. And I guess I should give you some background. He killed my mom and I was a part of it. I was not physically there but I knew and I helped him. I was, you know, going through the motions of what was being done. But mentally and emotionally, I don't think I was fully there. I don't think I was fully getting it."

"It was emotional manipulation," Russo said. "It is all so scary romantic for a fifteen year old girl to have some guy who is so in love with her that he is going to kill himself because he can't be with her. She has no one in her life to say 'this guy is a loser nutcase.' There isn't anyone that can talk sense to her. So she falls for the emotional manipulation of a highly disturbed but cunning con man."

Billy had convinced the depressed Nicole that her mother was an obstacle to both hers and his happiness.

"I really just did whatever I could to maintain that relationship because I didn't want to lose that," Nicole said. "I didn't want to lose him. And I quickly learned how it would go if I didn't always do everything that he wanted me to do. At that point...you know, getting to be fifteen...sixteen years old...I would fight more with my mom and there was a lot more to fight about, especially with, you know, this relationship that I was having with this kid."

THE FINAL PLAN

The couple tried different methods to murder Jeanne Domenico.

First they tried to poison Jeanne's coffee. The teens had placed Dimetapp, Benadryl and other drugs into Jeanne's coffee creamer in the refrigerator.

Jeanne used the creamer but didn't die and evidently remained ignorant of the plot on her life. The teens then added bleach to the creamer, wanting to strengthen the amount of poison. It was unclear in a court affidavit if Jeanne ever drank from the spiked creamer again.

The next idea was to set Nicole's mattress on fire with a candle. That idea didn't work because the bedding was made of fire retardant material.

It is unclear how the teens planned to fire up the mattress, whether they sneaked into her Nicole's bedroom and tried to fire up the mattress while she slept.

The third idea was to blow up the fuel oil tank in Jeanne's house. The teens had tied two ropes together which would serve as a wick. Their idea was to set fire to the rope which would then ignite a fire from the fuel tank. This idea was of course unsuccessful.

"These were hair-brained schemes from the start," Russo said, "particularly the fuel tank episode. What is interesting is that these are passive attacks. There is no face to face encounter with the mother, they just really want her gone. But it does show how these were test-runs of sorts. Sullivan was working up his nerve to do something violent. Nicole was building up her psyche. With each unsuccessful dry run, their determination and focus to do the job became greater until finally they realized that physical violence would be the only alternative."

THE ATTACK

The couple decided that Sullivan would do the killing. Nicole waited in the car at a local 7-Eleven where he mother worked part time to make ends meet. She wanted to wait there because she hated her home so much. Her boyfriend obliged, and entered the home of Jeanne Domenico between the hours of six and seven in the evening, waiting for her to come home from work.

The plan was for Billy to kill Jeanne by hitting her on the back of her head with a baseball bat.

Nicole waited anxiously in the car for an extended period of time then began to get worried as to why Sullivan was taking so long.

"Nicole called him and asked him what was taking so long," Wilson said. "Jeanne began getting upset that Nicole wasn't home and kept saying 'where is she? Tell her to come home.'"

Nicole heard her mother's voice on the other end of her cell phone telling her to "come home."

As became her habit, she did not listen to her mother.

"Sullivan did not attack Jeanne immediately," Russo said. "Again, he needed that fuel to add to his fire. So he confronted Jeanne, asking her why they kept refusing them to be together. Jeanne would speak logically like any adult would. She's underage. She's still in school. Of course, none of this would get into the head of Sullivan."

Jeanne made the mistake of turning her back on the young man. He then hit her across the back with the baseball bat.

"It looks as if Jeanne tried to get out of the kitchen door," Wilson said. "Billy started grabbing kitchen knives and attacking Jeanne with the steak knives from the state clock in the kitchen."

The attack was, in a word, brutal.

Sullivan stabbed Jeanne numerous times near her heart and stomach. He stabbed with such ferocity that the blade broke off the knife and he had to retrieve another. Then he stabbed her eight times in the throat.

"A number of the steak knives snapped off during the course of the attack," Wilson said.

According to later testimony by Sullivan, Jeanne managed to get a hold of one of the knives and tried to fight back. At this point, however, she is stunned and bleeding. Sullivan realizes that he is in trouble and goes in to finish the job.

Sullivan stabs her repeatedly as Jeanne tries to get away. A blade enters her lung.

"I'm done," were Jeanne's final words.

He then changed his clothes and cleaned the blood off. He then went back to Nicole, telling her to go inside the house to check for any weapons that he may have left behind. He also told her to get a towel.

The murder complete, Sullivan returned to the vehicle and announced that he had done the deal.

The couple, however, had a deal. It was now time for Nicole to do her part. She would help clean up the evidence left behind.

"The fact that she could go and clean up after Billy had killed her mother," Wilson said. "She had to have hit her mother with the door. And then she had to have stepped over her body to clean up for her boyfriend. That she was able to do that was chilling to do me."

Nicole took a cloth and began clean up her mother's blood from the kitchen floor.

"The fact that a psychopath like Sullivan was able to stab Jeanne to death isn't the most blood curdling aspect of this case," Russo said. "The really scary part is how Nicole was able to go back into that house, see her mother laying in a pool of blood on the kitchen floor, then begin to do her end of the bargain, which was to clean up after her boyfriend. The amount of psychological and emotional disconnect here is chilling."

The two then hid the evidence in the outskirts around town before going to a shopping mall in order for Sullivan to purchase new clothes.

Hours after the killing, Nicole finally began to realize the gravity of what has taken place. She realizes that she and Billy were not going off to "see the world." Her best friend, her mother was gone forever.

Jeanne's body would be discovered by her boyfriend later that evening and he quickly called the police. At around 10:15 p.m., Sergeant William Moore and Detective Shawn Hill saw Sullivan and Nicole approach the crime scene.

"They were cocky enough to think they could outwit the cops," Russo said. "By approaching the crime scene and acting all innocent, not knowing what happened, they thought they would deflect attention away from themselves. It really shows you how dumb these two kids were."

The police then stated the teens would have to be separated for an interview. Nicole protested, stating that Sullivan would not know how to get to the police station. The police informed her that they would take him there themselves.

"This is when things start to go haywire in their heads," Russo said. "Nicole is getting nervous, knowing that they will be questioned separately and face the prospect of not having their stories straight. These two were not exactly forward thinking individuals."

The two waited for the police cruisers to arrive and made conversation with Detective Moore. The detective noted that Sullivan did most all of the talking and admitted that he did not like police officers, stating that he had been charged before with crimes he did not commit.

Moore informed Sullivan that he would be given a "fair shake" in the questioning.

Sullivan, however, kept talking. He informed the detective that he had been shopping for souvenirs with Nicole that day and talked about Jeanne's relationship with Nicole. The detective said that Sullivan paced back and forth and then sat down on the trunk of his car.

Twelve minutes later, Detective Linehan arrived on the scene, making contact with both Nicole and Sullivan. Linehan noticed how nervous and "jumpy" Sullivan was. Linehan told Sullivan to "relax" and then the teen explained that he suffered from anxiety but did not need medication. He told the police that he had "no problem" to come to the station for questioning.

Linehan sat with Sullivan in the back seat of the squad car as they headed back to the station. Both of the teens were having casual conversations with the officers but after being questioned separately, they both admitted their involvement, leading police to the locations where they had disposed of the evidence.

"Both of the teenage lovers wilted under the police interrogations," Russo said. "She immediately ratted out Sullivan as the killer while he did the same to her. There was no loyalty for one another while under the police questioning."

Sullivan would be convicted of first degree murder, sentenced to life without parole.

Sullivan, however, did not let his Lothario ways go to rust in jail. He wrote love letters to a girl named Monique Teal who was then sixteen. This occurred while Sullivan was awaiting trial and later Teal's testimony was used in court.

Teal, using a pen name of Monique Sullivan in her love letters to Sullivan, had agreed to a date to marry the now twenty-year old murderer. Teal's mother, however, found out about the letters and forbade him to call or write.

"He just laughed about it," she said. "He said that no matter what my mom would say or do that nothing could keep us away from each other."

"You see him trying the same techniques on Teal," Russo said. "The immediate declarations of love. The flowery language. The idea of them against the world. In Teal's case, however, her mother put a stop to it."

Sullivan admitted to the Jeanne Domenico killing in one of his letters to her, Teal would reveal, although she didn't read from the letter in court. She said she obeyed Sullivan's demands and threw that letter away.

JAIL LIFE

Nicole Kasinskas would plead guilty to second-degree murder.

"My original sentence was forty years to life," Nicole said. "It is now thirty-seven years and a half to life based on a plea that if I acquired my GED I would get two and a half years off. I don't mark days off on my calendar. I don't do those types of things. This is my life now and I want to live it. I don't want to just look at it as one day down closer to my real life. Like this is my real life. I smile a lot and I live a lot and I'm happy a lot and I just prefer it that way rather than get lost in the sadness of it because you can. And I have. But if I...if I can choose not to...if I can be stronger than than then I want to. And it makes me feel freer. It makes me feel that I have more control of my life."

"Her life as a promising honor roll student at fifteen years old with her mother who loved her very much," Wilson said. "She lost her entire life. And for what?"

"I had no goals. I had no hopes and dreams, you know? You need to have your own hobbies and friends and stuff. Outside the relationship, there needs to be that balance. I just never had that, I never figured that out."

"Maybe if someone had said something like, 'I see you, I see that there's more to you than this and I want to see more of you. I'm here for you. I care about you.' I mean everyone needs help, everyone needs support."

KILLER BABYSITTER : THE TRUE STORY OF CHRISTINE FALLING

135

DIANE ULLMER

It is said that cats have nine lives, most understand this as a mildly clever metaphor for the preternatural ability of felines to land on their feet.

The mentally challenged Christine Falling took this saying quite literally, so much so that during her formative years she would regularly take cats up to the top of the highest buildings in her Perry, Florida neighborhood and dropped them off over the roof.

Sometimes she would strangle them instead.

Most of the people that came in contact with her would walk away shaking their head in disbelief at her ignorance.

Stupidity would prove to be dangerous, however, as Christine would seek employment as a babysitter.

Tragically, she would soon graduate from killing cats to killing children.

Christine Laverne Slaughter was born on the 12th of March in 1963 to a poor and dysfunctional working class family in Florida. From an early age it was clear that she had a great deal of cards stacked against her, which included a large appetite, frontal lobe epilepsy (for which she had to take regular and powerful medication to prevent an epileptic attack or seizure) and an astonishingly low IQ.

Still, no one would notice the little girl walking down the street cradling different cats.

"She killed the cats," forensic psychologist Paula Orange said. "Because she wanted to take her rage out on something. Anything. Any small animal would do. She wanted to have power over life and death over something as she didn't have any power in her own life."

Both of her parents were poor and they would fight often. Some were petty outbursts while others turned violent. When these altercations turned physical, and they often did, the police would be called, time after time, typically with little repercussions.

Her father would also sexually abuse her in addition to administering daily beatings when she didn't please him.

"The loss of innocence came early for Christine," Orange said. "Her father was a sick pervert, pulling her into the bedroom as she was watching cartoons."

One day, after one of the daughter and father's incestuous meetings, Christine's father became suddenly irate and began to beat her with a bottle. Her mother rushed her to the hospital where she told an investigating officer that Christine had been in a car accident.

"A car done run her over," Christine's mother said. "I didn't get the license plate."

The physician that examined the little girl felt otherwise. The injuries were clearly caused by blunt force trauma but the police did not follow up.

"Christine and her sister were under the radar of child protective services," Orange said. "And they remained that way for a long, long time. The child protective service was not set up the way now. Christine was savaged as a young child. Like so many victims of sexual abuse, her wiring would change and she would be destined to some kind of tragic life, taking people along for the ride."

According to Christine sister, Carol, their parents were so aloof and detached from the rearing of their children that on one trip to the local supermarket, their mother, Ann Slaughter, simply decided to abandon them there. Shortly thereafter both girls were adopted by Dolly and Jesse Falling (thus adopting the last name over Slaughter). Dolly Falling always dreamed of having children but, due to physiological complications was completely incapable of doing so – for her, the sight of the Slaughter children was a godsend. Jesse Falling knew the Slaughters well and also readily accepted them into his home. However, this newest sanctuary was anything but, for not only did Christine's mental issues cause a lot of problems but there were also rumors that Jesse Falling would regularly sexually abuse the children.

These allegations were investigated and Jesse was twice arrested for allegedly sexually assaulting Carol. The allegations were never proven, however, and he served no jail time.

At the age of nine, both Christine and her sister Carol were taken from the Fallings. They were taken to a child care center located in Orlando following the intervention of a local pastor who worried about the two girls.

The Fallings hesitated with the request but eventually gave in to the advice of the pastor. Their new was called The Great Oaks Village of Orlando, a home for neglected and downtrodden children. Christine liked her new home despite making everyone around her feel awkward. She would often give her fellow children "strange looks" and walk the halls with a vacant gaze.

Christine also developed a habit of bursting out into sudden fits of rage that seemed wholly unprovoked, distressing the other children and caretakers. She was also extremely antisocial and would often move off to sit by herself, hardly ever conversing with any of the other residents of her new home.

"Her rage came about whenever she couldn't deal with something," Orange said. "Like a child crying over a broken toy or spilled milk. The problem was Christine was older now and still exhibiting child-like behavior."

At the age of only fourteen, Christine would marry a twenty-three-year-old man at the behest of her parents. The union was anything but a happy one, often devolving into heated shouting matches and violence.

Christine did not hold back during their physical altercations and on one occasion hurled a thirty-pound stereo at her beau's head.

They would separate only six weeks of wedded "bliss."

After the break-up, Christine would psychologically deteriorate even further. During this period of manic distress, Christine visited the hospital over fifty times yet the physician would never find anything wrong with her.

Nothing except hypochondria.

And yet, time after time, Christine continued to return to the hospital, every time with new and increasingly bizarre and outlandish symptoms.

ADULTHOOD

Christine grew into an oversized Baby Huey looking character as she grew old. She had a bulbous forehead and a child-like way of talking. Uneducated, she applied for jobs in restaurants and schools but was rejected. She held some menial jobs but could not last long in conventional employment.

Her epilepsy, child-like mannerisms and below average intelligence disqualified her from just about every line of work. Luckily, she was well liked by her neighbors, who saw in her an affable childish innocence, and she quickly found herself regularly assuming the role of babysitter for the community.

She had seemingly finally found her niche, gaining a reputation among the community as a caring and reliable babysitter.

"Her smile was disarming," Orange said. "Her demeanor was disarming. No one would suspect her of anything. In fact, she looked like someone who needed babysitting herself."

But on February 25th, 1980, everything changed.

Christine was asked to look after a playful child named Cassidy Johnson, a neighbor's kid.

Cassidy's parents left their child in the care of Christine without any trepidation. The child seemed to like Christine and they looked like they could get along.

A few hours later, however, Cassidy fell ill and was rushed to the doctor.

The initial diagnosis was that the child was suffering from encephalitis, the severe inflammation of the brain which is typically a condition brought on by very serious cerebral infections. The child languished in feverish oblivion for three terrifying days before dying.

The coroner's examination would reveal something else, however. The cause of the brain swelling was blunt force trauma to the girl's skull.

Only one person could have been responsible.

Christine Falling.

INTERROGATION

Christine tried to lie her way through the police questioning. She told them that the child had fallen from the crib and hit her head on the floor.

The police were not in the slightest convinced by there was no evidence to be had and no one else to corroborate or contest Falling's tale. The doctor who had attended to the child was suspicious himself and wrote a letter describing his misgivings to the cops.

His letter was lost and the case soon became forgotten...

MOVING TIME

Christine was smart enough to realize that she should not stick around. She moved to Lakeland, Florida which was becoming a bustling business center.

Christine settled in, finding a place to live in a trailer park where she would spend her days watching television and milling around outside her trailer, smoking and greeting passersby.

She returned to do the only work she knew; babysitting.

Finding work with the unsuspecting Davis family, she began watching over their four-year-old son Jeffery.

"Christine did have a playful side," Orange said. "She entered the Davis home and immediately to a shine to the young Jeffery. She pretended like she was a monster and began tickling the young boy. Jeffery's parents had no reason to suspect that she would do harm to him. Christine was a little slow but was young and could project a sweet persona when she needed."

Hours later, however, Jeffery's mother would come home to see Christine standing over her young son with a glass of Kool-Aid.

Her son was not breathing.

"What happened?" Jeffery's mother screamed.

"He stopped breathing."

"Don't just stand there," she screamed again. "Call an ambulance!"

Jeffery would be pronounced dead on arrival at the hospital.

An autopsy was performed but the cause of death was found to be a pre-existing heart condition which caused the life-sustaining organ to expand to an extremely unhealthy size. Upon further inspection, however, the coroner determined that the heart inflammation was not enough to cause this kind of sudden death. Failing to discover any other notable injuries or oddities of the child's physiology, the case was chalked up as a mysterious death.

Three days later, however, Christine would by hired to look after a young boy named Joseph Spring. His parents would be going to the funeral of the young Jeffery.

They had no idea that Christine was responsible for Jeffery's death.

Christine followed the same modus operandi as she did with young Jeffery. She was immediately able to charm the child with her own child-like qualities. She saw that the boy was interested in trucks and started to play "demolition derby" with him. His parents were satisfied that the child would be safe in her care and went to the funeral of Jeffery, their nephew who had been killed by their babysitter.

Joseph's parents left and after a few hours, the boy fell. He began crying and screaming which set off Christine.

"She couldn't handle frustration of any kind," Orange said. "She would pace back and forth, telling the boy to 'shush' but of course he doesn't listen. She can't handle it."

Christine experienced auditory hallucinations when her frustrations reached a peak. The voices in her head would tell her to 'kill' and 'make the child quiet.' She could not differentiate between the real voices and the voices in her head.

So she grabbed the nearest blanket and began suffocating the young boy.

"She was schizophrenic," Orange said. "You combine that with her low IQ and it is the recipe for disaster if she is watching a young child. She cannot parse out her rational thoughts from the voices in her head. This would lead to tragic consequences."

Like before, the coroner was puzzled by the death of a young and healthy boy. He speculated that

the cause of death might very well have been some undocumented, possibly new kind of viral infection. This theory would also account for the death of Jeffery Davis as well as Joseph since neither of them bore any marks of violence. Once again the coroner closed the case, dismissing it as a complete mystery.

"No one suspected Christine of anything," Orange said. "Her dumb and sweet persona actually worked in her favor. Nobody could suspect any malice to come out of her. She would smile and come across like an overgrown child. She didn't fit the mold of a child killer. On the surface, she had no sinister aspect about her."

Christine's reign of terror continued to go on unchecked as she moved to the town of Perry. This go around, however, she would become a caretaker rather than a babysitter. An elderly man named Wilbur Swindle needed someone to look after him and find a willing candidate in the smiling Christine.

On her first day of employment, however, the old man would be found dead.

Once again, the coroner would drop the ball, dismissing the old man's death due to a heart attack brought on by the failing health of old age.

There was no police inquiry.

"The killing of Wilbur Swindle seemed to be an anomaly in Christine's pattern of murder," Orange said. "For whatever reason, she had targeted young children. So the killing of Swindle looked to be a murder of opportunity. He probably did or said something to upset her. He was old and feeble and could easily be smothered down by the obese Christine."

TIME AWAY

Some time passed and Christine was contacted by her step-sister Geneva Daniels. Geneva had an eight-month-old daughter. They had not seen each other in awhile and Geneva invited Christine to go on a shopping trip.

On the way home, Geneva remembered that she needed some diapers. She parked outside the local store and ran in for only a minute.

She made the mistake of leaving the crying baby with Christine.

Moments later, an ear-piercing scream could be heard from the car. The louder the child screamed, the more agitated Christine became.

"Once again, her low frustration threshold kicked in," Orange said. "She simply never learned how to handle a stressful situation. What would seem like a mundane situation to a normal person, a baby crying, would seem like a life or death scenario to Christine. The more the baby cried, the less control she felt. Then she had to lash out."

She placed the baby's fuzzy blanket over its mouth and held it there until she stopped crying.

Her step-sister returned to the car only to find her eight-month-old baby girl in a lifeless heap in the arms of Christine.

Christine herself was crying, flailing her arms and hyperventilating.

"She stopped breathing," Christine said.

Her step-sister didn't suspect Christine at all.

Neither did the police.

"That is one of the reasons why Christine was able to commit these murders," Orange said. "She mastered the art of smothering, particularly with a loose material. It doesn't leave behind any marks or clues. It simply blocks the airways and the coroners are left grasping at straws."

JUSTICE AT LAST...

Christine's long, lengthy string of supernatural luck in avoiding suspicion came to a bitter and crushing end in the year of 1982.

Christine would meet a family who employed her to watch their ten-week-old son named Travis Coleman.

Travis would die under her care but initially, they held no suspicions toward Christine.

The coroner's exam would reveal that the child's death had not been some viral infection or cerebral swelling, but rather a strangulation!

Christine would go immediately to the hospital and check herself in. Her hypochondriac tendencies kicking in, she demanded that doctors find out what was wrong with her. She insisted that she was passing along a virus that was killing the children.

The physicians would find nothing wrong with her physically.

Finally, Christine told the doctor to call the police.

"I have something I want to tell them," she said.

Christine did not lie this time when faced with police questioning. She said she had killed her child using a method she described as "smotheration."

She then confessed to killing the other children using similar methods.

"Christine probably wanted to be caught at this point," Orange said. "She would confess while she was at the hospital. She wanted the burden off her back. Whatever it was inside her that was forcing her to kill those children, she wanted herself to be committed. In one moment of lucidity she probably realized what a danger she was to everyone around her."

When the police pressed the young woman as to why she had done such a heinous series of deeds she responded flatly that she had heard voices in her head.

These voices told her to use "soft, thick pillows and blankets" which were the reasons why there were no discernible and incriminating marks on her victims.

Christine spoke openly of hearing strange and seductive voices telling her to "kill the baby, kill the baby, kill the baby, kill the baby!"

These words would be repeated in her head, over and over like some kind of demonic mantra.

"I don't know why I done what I done," Christine said. "The way I done it, I seen it done on TV shows. I had my own way, though. Simple and easy. No one would hear them scream."

CONVICTION

Christine was able to avoid the death penalty but was instead sentence to a life term of imprisonment with the prospect for possible parole via joint committee decision in 2007. However, in 2006 the committee came to an early decision.

She had been behaving badly in prison, engaging in unpredictable and violent outbursts. The court then dismissed her chance for parole in its entirety.

The committee judged Christine to be a threat to the public (specifically children for obvious reasons) and declared that the safest and most forward thinking course of action is to keep her imprisoned to fulfill the rest of her term.

Christine Falling remains in dark and clanking confines of the well known Homestead Prison Complex of Miami and Dade County in the state of Florida.

Her story is perhaps a penultimate warning about the dangers of undiagnosed mental health issues and childhood abuse. If the history of such heinous crime in America tells us, it's that the combination of mental frailty and a past of physical and emotional ill-treatment is a cocktail that is not just dangerous, but deadly.

CHRISTINA RIGGS

Christina Riggs had all the drugs she needed.

She had filled her prescription for the anti-depressant Elavil at the pharmacy. She had stolen morphine and potassium chloride from the hospital. Now all she had to do was follow through.

"Kids," she bellowed out from the living room table. "Vitamins!"

The two sleepy-eyed children emerged from their bedroom. Christina gave them a small amount of Elavil, dropping the pill in their mouth and watching them drink it down with a cup of water.

A few minutes later, she carried them both back to bed.

Looking down at her two young children, she began to sob.

Shelby, just two years old, in her pink jumper. Justin, five years old, in his white pajamas with battleship designs.

I have to do this. Things will only get worse for them.

THE GREATEST TABOO

Christina Marie Riggs was twenty-six years when she decided to kill her children.

"A mother is supposed to protect her own children," Riggs' Defense Attorney John Wesley Hall Jr. said. "And here she didn't and it doesn't make sense. Two defenseless children that didn't know what was coming."

After Christina sedated her children, she proceeded with her plan of injecting them with potassium chloride. She knew that the drug was administered for lethal injection executions and would stop the heart within minutes.

What she didn't know was that the drug had to be administered in a diluted form. If it is injected without any dilution, it will burn through the skin then burst through the vein.

Ignorant of the consequences, Christina injected the lethal cocktail into her son Justin first.

She wanted a painless death. She did not want her children to go through life suffering like she did.

But then her son woke up screaming.

The potassium chloride she injected was binding and burning through his blood vessel linings.

He cried and cried and wouldn't stop.

Christina began crying herself...

CHILDHOOD TRAUMA

Christina Riggs had a troubled childhood growing up in Oklahoma City, OK.

She was separated from her brothers and sisters after her parent's divorce. Raised alone by her mother, she detailed in a prison diary sexual abuses that took place in her childhood.

She wrote how her stepbrother sexually abusing her from the age of seven to thirteen. At the age of thirteen, she was molested by a neighbor as well.

By the time she entered her teenage years, Christina was obese, using food as an emotional outlet. She also began abusing alcohol and marijuana.

"She indulged in overeating because she didn't want to appear attractive," forensic psychologist Paula Orange said. "That behavior was part of a psychological response to being molested. 'If I become fat and ugly then he won't want me anymore.' No one will bother me, no one will hurt me."

In her teenage years, however, Christina began to use sex as a way to get what she wanted, which was love.

"It isn't uncommon for abused young women to become very promiscuous," Orange said. "It is learned behavior. She became defective, if you will, and should have gotten help. Unfortunately, this is not a good recipe for someone who wants to have a healthy stable relationship and raise children."

"I felt that no boy liked me because of my weight," Christina wrote in her journal. "So I became sexually promiscuous because I thought that was the only way I could have a boyfriend."

She became pregnant by the age of sixteen but gave the baby boy up for adoption.

After high school, Christina went to a vocational school to become a licensed practical nurse (LPN). She obtained employment as a home care nurse and then later worked full-time at a VA hospital.

Her dating life remained steady albeit unsuccessful. She went from one man to the next, dating a Navy ensign named Jon Riggs and a bouncer before meeting Timothy Thompson. Thompson was an Air Force private at Tinker Air Force Base.

Three years after her first child, Christina would become pregnant with Timothy's baby. She informed Timothy her pregnancy the day before he was to be discharged from the Air Force.

Timothy, however, did not take the news well. He would not accept responsibility and moved back to his native Minnesota.

"Chrissy's luck with men was about zero to nothing," Carol Thomas, Christina's mother said.

But while her relationship ended with Timothy, Christina hooked back up with Jon Riggs who returned home after being on leave with the Navy.

"It was great," Christina wrote. "He felt the baby's first kick. As far as he was concerned, it was his baby."

Justin Thomas was born on June 7th, 1992.

"As I held Justin in my arms and looked into his little face, I became so scared," Christina wrote. "Would I be a good Mom? Could I give him all he needed?"

Riggs would move in with Christina and the two hoped for the best. Christina would become pregnant again and the couple would marry in July of 1993.

But misfortune would strike again as Christina would suffer a miscarriage on her wedding night.

The marriage would go south from there as Christina alternated between being depressed to having suicidal thoughts. She blamed her mental state on her birth control medication and a doctor gave her the anti-depressant Prozac.

The medication worked for a while but then Christina inexplicably stopped taking the drug. She kept her sadness to herself and didn't want to burden others with her problems.

"She's always been that way," Christina's mother said. "If I pushed her hard she might get mad and tell me what was going on."

By 1994, Christina would become pregnant and deliver a healthy baby girl in December named Shelby. This would mark the high point of Christina's life as "Sissie" and "Bubbie", the two nicknames for her children, brought immeasurable joy into her life.

She would write that it was the happiest time of her life as both she and Jon cried when they held their new baby in their arms. Things were happy for once in her life.

Christina continued to work as a vocational nurse and was assigned to work at a triage station which served to help the victims of the Oklahoma City Federal Building terrorist bombing. She would suffer post-traumatic stress disorder as a result. Later at her trial, the prosecuting attorneys would argue that the hospital had no record of Christina serving after the bombing. This may be nitpicking as authorities were lenient with record keeping during that urgent situation.

STRESS AND STRAIN

A year later, the couple would move to Sherwood, Arkansas to be closer to Christina's mother, Carole.

Carole worked as a food service worker at Baptist Hospital and Christina was able to find a job there as well, once again working as a licensed practical nurse.

The children go on to have ailments that would stress out the already fragile Christina. Shelby would have chronic ear infections that made doctor visits a routine thing. Justin was diagnosed with attention deficit disorder and his hyper nature would grate on the nerves of his parents.

Financial difficulties and the stress of running a family would put a strain on the marriage and the couple would eventually divorce. Her husband, Jon Riggs, had a volatile temper that he eventually took out on the young Justin. Jon would punch Justin in the abdomen with such force that the young boy had to go to the emergency room.

Jon would then abandon the family.

"Justin would say, 'My Daddy hurt me, and then he went away,' " Christina's mother recalled.

Christina would receive limited child support from Jon and had to work long hours to provide for her family. The more hours she worked, the more she had to pay for daycare which proved to be a daily traumatic event.

Shelby would cry as Christina would leave her at the facility.

"She was beating on the glass, yelling, 'Mama! Mama!' " Christina recalled.

Despite her increased efforts, Christina could not get ahead financially. She began writing bad checks. Bills remained unpaid. Car insurance. Car registration. Lights and utilities.

"I started out in a boat with a small hole," Christina said. "But the hole kept getting bigger, and no matter how hard you bail, you keep sinking. I was tired and I gave up. Suicide seemed like the only thing."

A HISTORY OF MENTAL ILLNESS

Christina had a cousin that killed herself. Her mother had also tried to kill herself when Christina was a baby. Her grandmother was committed to a mental institution.

But Christina would outdo them all in one fateful night.

"Just speaking in general," Orange said. "When mothers kill their children they do not poison them. In the case of Christina, she was applying what she thought would be a lethal injection."

But even with a history of mental illness in the family, nobody could have predicted how the sweet and caring Christina could commit such a heinous crime.

"Chrissy always wanted to help people," Christina's sister, Elizabeth Nottingham said. "She was always helping someone."

But Nottingham had some valuable psychological insight on her sister. She was a mental health counselor and had been close to Christina.

She wanted to know what drove her sister to kill her own children. After her sister's arrest, she began fishing around her house, looking for some kind of clue, a sign that everyone had missed.

"I was almost hoping to find that she wasn't a good parent," Nottingham said. "Then I could be mad at her. You know, I went through her house with a fine toothed comb. All the chemicals were locked away. The food was in the refrigerator. Even pictures of their fathers was in their room above each of their beds. She was great with the kids."

MORE TROUBLE WITH MEN

What Christina's sister would find out was that she simply could not find a decent man. That one relationship where everything would be ideal.

After her divorce from Jon, Christina would enter into another relationship which again would not go well.

"The guy didn't just break her heart," Nottingham said. "But took her credit card. I mean, it's one thing to have someone dump you, it's another to have someone rip you off and leave you destitute too."

After this break-up, Christina would sit at her dining room table both broke and broken-hearted. She had no man in her life. She had no means to pay her family's bills.

Seeing only dark lights ahead, Christina would lapse into a deep depression. She went to her doctor again who prescribed her more Prozac which used irregularly.

"She may have stopped taking the Prozac when she killed the babies," Orange said. "When someone just stops that medication cold-turkey it can have some side effects like increased irritability, irrational mood changes, and an even deeper depression."

"So she had the perfect storm brewing," Nottingham said. "She had depression, she had all of these personal failures. You know, people talk about having rainy days and Mondays. And in fact 'Rainy days and Mondays' was the CD that was in her CD player."

BACK TO THAT FATEFUL NIGHT

Christina had to kill herself. Her emotional bank account had been overdrawn for years.

But she couldn't stand the thought of leaving her children alone.

"If she left the kids behind," Hall Jnr said. "She was afraid that the children would be separated, go to their father's, for instance, and be split up."

"She just thought there was no other way out," Nottingham said. "She thought that no one else would take care of her kids. And that they would be better off, in her mind, she was saving them from future sadness."

With Justin screaming in pain, Christina panicked. She began sobbing but whatever remain of her maternal instinct kicked in and she tried to inject him with morphine.

Toxicology reports didn't reveal whether or not she did this.

But what she did do was suffocate her young son with a pillow. Sobbing, she then did the same deed to her baby daughter, Shelby.

Shaking with adrenaline and grief, Christina wobbled on shaky legs back to her living room. She took out her bottle of Elavil, an anti-depressant, and swallowed the remaining twenty-eight pills. Her nerves calming, she tried injecting the potassium chloride into her own arm.

The chemical burn right through her vein, collapsing it.

The drugs began taking effect and Christina fainted to the floor, hoping her nightmare would finally end.

THE DAY AFTER

The lethal mixture had burned a half-inch hole into Christina's arm. She didn't show up for work the next day and her mother called her cell phone and land line repeatedly.

Worried that she received no response, Carole drove to Christina's apartment and let herself in.

To her horror, she thought everyone was dead, including Christina.

"All I could do was turn around and around and scream and holler, 'No. No. No.' There's no way to describe how I felt."

Frantic, she called 911 and yelling into the phone, "My daughter and babies are dead."

Paramedics would arrive.

The children were dead.

But the medics were able to resuscitate Christina. She was transported to the intensive care unit and was kept under guard by the police.

"I had to do it so I wouldn't leave them behind," Christina was overheard saying in her hospital room. The treating physician, Dr. Jim Rice, would later testify that Christina as "combative at times" and "just incoherent and not really making any sense."

As soon as Christina became reasonably coherent, she was taken to the police station for booking.

THE INTERROGATION

On November 6th, 1997, Christina was interrogated by a Detective Jones and Detective Sharon Williams.

"Christina, what we are doing is investigating the death of your two babies. Do you want to tell us what happened?" Jones asked.

"I killed them," Christina said, crying.

"What did you say?"

"I said-"

"Did you say you killed them?"

"I'm sorry."

"How did you go about doing that?" Jones asked.

"I got some bottles and stuff from here...I need a cigarette...Darvocet."

"Are you saying that you got some medicine from the hospital?"

Christina nodded.

"Christina, how did you do it? Did you give them an injection? Did you give them a shot?"

"I tried to ... and ... I did it with Justin because I figured with him being the oldest one that he would give me more problems. So, I tried it with him and I thought it would just stop his heart. But it hurt. Oh, he said it hurt ...It didn't work, he just kept calling, 'Momma! Momma! Momma!' I just figured it was too late now because I had no place to turn back to. I cleaned out my checking account and gave my mother all the money I had."

"Christina, why did you do this?" Jones asked.

"Because I wanted to die," Christina said, crying again. "But I didn't want to die and leave my kids behind or for them to be a burden to somebody else. I didn't want them to think I didn't love them and I didn't want them to grow up separately because they have two different Daddies. And I knew if I passed away they would be fighting my Mother for custody and I didn't want that for nobody."

"You felt like you were doing it for the kids' sake?"

"In a way, yeah... my piece of mind."

"Christina, did you really want to die?"

Christina didn't respond. She continued crying.

"And you felt it would be better if your children just die with you and ... were the children already dead before you took your medicine?"

"Yes."

"How long had they been dead before you took your medicine?"

"About twenty minutes."

"About twenty minutes?"

"That's because I drank and got up and smoked a cigarette and got back and sit for a minute and...I was like, 'Okay, I'm going to do it now. I can't turn back now because you've already killed Justin.' And ... so I did it."

"What time did you give them the medicine? Do you remember?"

"Justin about 10:15 or 10:30."

"10:15 or 10:30 in the morning?"

"No, in the evening."

"Oh, in the evening?"

"Last night."

"Okay."

"Then I smoked another cigarette and waited," Christina paused. "And suffocated Shelby."

"You suffocated Shelby? What did ... how did you suffocate her?"

"I put a pillow over her head."

"Okay, Did you ... Had you given her any medicine at all, or ... any of the Morphine or the Potassium Chloride?"

"I slipped them ... I made them drink half of an Elavil because I figured that would make them sleep a little bit better so that it wouldn't wake them."

"So, Shelby, you killed her with a pillow. You suffocated her. And what about the little boy. How did you do him?"

"I gave him the medicine and when it didn't work."

"You suffocated him too?"

"Yes."

"With a pillow? Were they fighting while you suffocated them?"

"Justin did. Shelby a little bit but not much," Christina began to cry again.

"When did you decide to do this, Christina? On what day did you decide to do this?"

"Uh ... the best I remember it was Sunday night or Saturday night because we was out talking and this and that and the other ... and they caught me."

"Who caught you?"

"I was depressed. I was thinking about what was going on in my life and that things aren't always working for me and..."

"When did you get those drugs from the hospital?"

"When? Yesterday."

"Yesterday? You mean the day that you killed them? Is that the day that you got the drugs? The last was it ... "

"Was it the last day that you worked at the hospital or the day before that? "I think ...""

"When you got ... "

"I got the drugs and I gave them to my kids. That's the only drugs that I had in my hand. And I know that there was three Valiums in a vial in there, but there wasn't enough to even cover the jar up and put it in my pocket and bring them home. And I know I should have thought better ... had somebody rinsing with me, but ... they were just what came home in my pockets."

"Did you know what you were going to do when you took the drugs from the hospital? Did you have intentions of giving them to your children? And how many days did you think about this before you killed your children?"

"About three weeks. Two weeks."

"Two or three weeks. In other words, you've been thinking about doing this for the last two or three weeks? What made you decide to just go ahead and do it?"

"I just can't take it no more."

"You couldn't take it anymore."

"I felt like I was out of control," Christina said.

"Did you just feel like your life was in a mess? Had you talked to anybody about this? Your Mom or anybody?"

"I've tried to talk to people about what I feel and what I think and they were just like, 'I don't have time right now. We'll do it some other time.' So, I just got to where I don't care anymore. I tried but they can't give me no help."

"So you just felt like nobody was listening to you? Okay, Christina ...Christina, do you have anything more to say about your babies or anything? "I wish I hadn't done it now."

Christina would then go on an incoherent ramble, explaining how she saw her mother riding down an escalator with a bunch of old people. The detectives, however, got the damning evidence they needed and ended the interrogation.

PRISON AND JAIL

Christina would find a hostile environment in prison. The majority of her fellow prisoners were women who were taken away from their children by force. They had contempt for Christina's crime.

One inmate spat in her face and her life was threatened.

Christina was then moved to an isolated cell where she remained until her trial.

She would be charged with two counts of first-degree murder which was punishable by death in the state of Arkansas.

"We tried to show that she was under extreme emotional disturbance," Hall Jr said. "To justify either not imposing the death penalty or hopefully finding her guilty of second-degree murder."

"I just hope that out of all her misery," Nottingham said. "The sadness of our family. That we can shed some light on the causes of this for other people and that maybe they'll be able to look at the symptoms and look at the situations and maybe intervene for someone else."

But the prosecuting attorney, as well as the community, believed that Christina was guilty of performing a selfish act, an act wherein she tried to free herself from motherhood.

The most damning evidence at the trial, aside from the interrogation tapes, would be the account of the physicians.

One doctor would testify that it would take three to six minutes to suffocate someone to death. Because of that time period, the jurors would be able to envision how Christina commit a willful act of murder. Christina had, in essence, a struggling toddler under her pillow for about three to six minutes...suffocating to death.

"They just wanted her to be evil," Nottingham said of the prosecuting attorney's intent. "It was easier that way."

"Essentially, what the jury saw was that she was self-centered," argued Pulaski Prosecuting Attorney Larry Jegley. "That she viewed the children as an inconvenience and an interference with what she wanted to pursue. She placed her interests above those of the children."

Jegley argued that Christina was a self-centered and premeditated murderer. He brought up the fact that she had locked the children up in the house (according to a neighbor) in order that she could go out to a Karaoke party. He urged the jury not to buy into her manipulation to feel sorry for her. "There were lots of people who have it worse than she did."

The jury would side with the prosecution and find Christina guilty after a very short deliberation period.

THE IRONY

Christina Riggs would be sentenced to death by lethal injection via potassium chloride...The same method that she used to try to kill her children and herself.

"It was a cruel irony that they finished what she started," Hall Jr said. "Almost the exact same way except she was strapped down to a table."

Christina would appeal the sentencing but did so with reluctance. She wanted to die.

"I'll be with my children and with God," Christina said. "I'll be where there's no more pain. Maybe I'll find some peace."

Her defense attorney John Wesley Hall Jr was allowed to witness the execution.

"You can see their face," Hall Jr said. "It allows them to say their last words. The face changes color as the drugs take effect. You turn gray. The skin turns gray. And it's rather shocking to watch it happen."

"She was so depressed that it became this black sheet over her eyes that she couldn't see through," Orange said. "She wanted to spare her own children from the kind of life that she had. She had lost complete hope and really over thought things. That's how her depression warped her. It warped her enough to think that she was doing her children a favor by killing them."

Christina was sent to death row and was haunted by the memories of her children. She openly stated that she tried "not to think about them" because when she did it was like someone "ripping them away from her all over again."

"A lot of regret," Christina said. "That's what goes through my mind, day-in, day-out. God's punishing me. He let me live so I would suffer."

Riggs was flown in from McPherson Jail to Cummins in order to prep for her execution. She would be administered the lethal injection at 9:28 PM CDT on May 2nd, 2000.

"No words can express just how sorry I am for taking the lives of my babies," Riggs said in a prepared statement. "No way I can make up for or take away the pain I have caused everyone who knew and loved them. I love you, my babies."